DISAPPEARING DOORS

DARLENE WALLACE

With

P.S. Anderson

Lipstick Publishing
www.lipstickpublishing.com

Lipstick Publishing,
118 Dewar Street,
Dunfermline, Fife.
Scotland KY12 8AA
www.lipstickpublishing.com
admin@lipstickpublishing.com

This paperback first edition 2006
First Published in Great Britain by
Lipstick Publishing 2006

ISBN: 1-904762-27-1
ISBN: 9781904762270

Darlene Wallace was born in the Midwest of America in the early sixties, to a working class family. She attended high school in a small town in Arkansas and graduated from her local junior college majoring in accounting.

She married, but eventually escaped a very violent relationship, and moved to Alaska where she found a job and continued her education.

While on a bicycle trip she was brutally attacked by two men hired by her ex-husband to kill her.

After several years of rehabilitation, Darlene has finally managed to put this part of her life into this book 'Disappearing Doors.'

She has adopted two boys who are the light of her life, and she spends much of her time and resources with the 'National Domestic Violence Centres of America'.

Late in 1996, Darlene contacted P.S. Anderson, who owns River's Bend Literary Agents, Inc. in Oklahoma. Eventually, the two women agreed to work together to make Darlene's story known.

Darlene sent Patricia her story on tape, and Patricia began to fashion the story into a book. This book has had many lives, and changed many times. It is now the book that

you see here ...

Disappearing Doors

*** Darlene has requested that a portion of her proceeds from the book, be given to:
'The National Domestic Violence' UK Charity Refuge: www.refuge.org.uk
'National Domestic Violence Centre of America' Charity
www.ndvh.org

DEDICATION

I would like to dedicate this book to all those who believed in me and helped me, and above all, those who believe that life can be better ...

CONTENTS

Introduction

I don't remember when exactly I first came to grips with the real facts of what was happening to my life. Perhaps it was the day that I was sitting at my desk in the doctor's office, and overheard a mother explaining to the doctor that her thirteen-year-old child was pregnant by the minister of their church. Perhaps it was when my husband beat my little brother so badly that I had to take him to the hospital, and get him out of my house before my husband killed him.

He wanted children; he wanted a house full of children. And I couldn't give him what he wanted, not even one. I have a medical condition. The doctor explained this to my husband, and he refused to believe it. I explained it to him, and he said that I was just lying, and trying to make him angry, angry enough to hurt me.

I was raised in a church that preaches that women are of no value, and I believed that. The preacher and the church told me that women couldn't own anything of value. That we must be led and instructed by our men, and we must never ever question them, because as *'Christ is the head of the Church, man is the head of the family.'*

I felt that I had my personal law laid out neatly before me. Oh, yes, I had independent moments, but believe me when you are around people like this, you forget them.

I have no idea why I didn't question my father, who set me up to marry this man that I did not love.

When I was a young girl, my mother took leave of the house with my two older siblings; I was left in charge of my father and my baby brother and of course the house. I was only eleven years old, and yet, I did everything I was supposed to. I kept up the housework, dinner was served on time, and my brother was never in a dirty diaper. I bought food from the store, and kept everyone on a schedule, including myself. So, what happened to me that made me feel so very, very worthless?

I wish I could tell you. I believe now that many people are the victims of circumstance. We are the victims of living in a controlling home, with people who control us through intimidation and threats. My father used my baby brother as a control.

"If you don't do what I say, I will ship your baby brother off to relatives far away, and you will never see him again."

My husband used my baby brother against me as well. "I'll kill that kid, and you will never see him alive again," he would shout at me.

All intimidators use the same tools and do the same things.

Control!

They find your weak spot and hold it over you.

I was so surprised when I attended the first day of college. I had been brainwashed into thinking that women were less than nothing. And here all around me were young women, wearing what they wanted to wear, cutting their hair, dyeing it even! I couldn't believe it. It was like I had dropped into a foreign country. *This can't be?* I thought to myself. Then I talked with several of these bright young women, and found out that they owned cars, they owned homes, and some of them even had more than one home. They were doing what they wanted and they were bright, eager participants in life.

Not exactly the portrait of the women that I saw every Sunday morning. The women who couldn't own a property in their own name. The women who couldn't drive a car alone, the women who had to wear black, grey, and dark print dresses. As if that wasn't enough, the dresses had to have high necks, and long sleeves, with the skirt dragging the floor when they walked. These were women who couldn't talk back, or in any way disgrace their 'men' folk. They definitely were not even of the same species.

I have often wondered why on earth I stayed with that man, and stayed in a relationship that was horrible beyond belief. Why did I stay married to Bobby Fulton? A man that I never loved, that I never even liked. And then on top of that, to suffer through everything that I did, to make that marriage work, when he tried so hard to make me his slave.

I know now that fear was my motivation. Fear was my motivation in dealing with my father; he threatened to take Johnny away from my care. Fear was my motivation for staying with Bobby; he threatened to murder my parents, to murder Johnny, and to finally murder me, if I dared to cross him in any way. In the end he almost got me, but, almost is not *did*. I was brainwashed into believing that me, as a woman, had no self worth. My husband told me over and over, that no other man would have me in his house. He continually told me that I was not worthy of any other person's consideration.

My mind told me different. I knew I was worth something. I did go to school. I did go to college. I did master classes. But then, the draining fog of doubt begins to cloud your mind. I began to believe that I would never find happiness, that no other man would ever want me. I began to believe that Bobby would kill me and my entire family if I tried to leave him. I even believed him when he told me that I wouldn't be able to support my little brother and myself if I left him. I began to believe the entire lie.

But that was then!!!

Chapter One

No Memories

The room looked odd. I blinked my eyes a couple of times and realised that I was in a room that was very sterile looking, certainly not my own room. I tried to move my head a little and found that it was impossible. I wondered where on earth I was. I tried to speak. I thought I wanted to ask someone what was going on, but I found that I had no voice. Things were fuzzy to me, and nothing was making any sense. What had happened to me?

I could hear voices, around me. They weren't making any sense. I moved my eyes as quickly as I could, trying to make some sort of contact with someone. I was scared. What if this is the way it was going to be? What if, I could never make contact with anyone ever again? And if I did, what if they couldn't understand me, or me them?

I was hearing the voices, but couldn't make out what they were saying. I couldn't work out if they were talking to me, or someone else. One of the voices sounded like a man, and he was talking very rapidly. Again I tried to move my head in the direction that I heard him speak, but I just couldn't move. There was something holding my head in a certain way, I didn't know why, or what it was. Then without warning, the man, whoever he was, got up from where he had been, and came over to my bed. He leaned over closer to me and I could make out he had a big weird smile on his face. There was nothing I wanted more than for him to get back from me. I desperately wanted him to get away from me. I had no idea who he was. I had no idea where I was. Worse than that, I suddenly realised, I had no idea who I was, or where I was either!

The man began to speak.

I had no idea how long I had been in this place, nor where I had come from, or how I got here.

The man with his face close to mine seemed to be yelling at me. I looked at him through very wide eyes as he spoke, "honey, you are awake! I can't believe it. How do you feel?"

"I ... I ... ahh ..." is all I could say. Then I realised the wildest thing. I couldn't figure out how to answer him. Oh, not that I didn't have an answer; I just didn't know how to tell him anything. I didn't know how to communicate with him. Finally, I strung out a few words: "What, ah, what, mm ... mm?" I stammered and stuttered, and about that time a nurse and a woman who must have been a doctor, ran into the room.

"She's awake," I heard one of them say.

"Sir, please let me get in there. I must see what's happening to her. She has been in a coma for more than a month, and now, well, please."

The older man moved out of the way, and a woman in a white coat drew near me. She looked at me, and asked: "Can you speak? I am Doctor Louise Norman. I've been taking care of you for the last month, well, since you arrived. And I wonder how you are?" I rolled my eyes around a little, and tried to ask where I was. I couldn't get the words out.

"Where ... where?" I asked.

"Oh, I guess you don't remember. You had an incident and you were thrown off the side of a cliff. You have been in a, um ... um, in a coma for the last few weeks and ..."

I must have looked terrified. I moved around a little and wanted very much to sit up.

3

"No, no. Don't move. Again, you don't know. We have had to do some surgery on you. In fact you have been operated on twice now. You are in a restraint so that you can't move. But, now you are awake we'll adjust that for you. You are going to be fine. Just lie there and rest," she said soothingly.

"Doctor, she is gonna be better? Right?" the man asked.

I rolled my eyes in his general direction and looked at him questioningly.

"Your parents have been here all this time. I know you can't look at them, but they have been right here," the nurse said with a smile.

"My parents?" I thought. I don't recognise any of these people. Maybe it's mom. Then, I don't know who mom is. In fact, I don't know who I am. God! God! What has happened to me?

I tapped my finger on the bed, and the nurse looked at me. Then she looked at the others. "I need to give her a morning bath now please, if you would all go out in the hall for a while, or perhaps you would like to go down to the restaurant and get something, maybe a coffee?"

The doctor took my pulse, and nodded in agreement as she walked around to the

4

other side of the bed and loosened something. Whatever she loosened now allowed me to move my head a little bit.

"I'm so sorry," the Doctor said. "I'm, em, rather used to you not being awake, so I've not had to tell you what I'm doing. I'm going to put new bandages on the wounds you have on your head, and then the nurse will take off some of the bandages from the rest of your body. She will give you a nice sponge bath and then redress the wounds. It is a bit uncomfortable for you, but it will be over soon."

She took the bandages from my head. I had gotten stiff from lying in one place and was hurting all over. I grunted.

"Did I hurt you?" She asked.

"No ... no." I replied.

"OK, then. Things are looking pretty good. We, um ... eh ... had to drill a hole in your skull Darlene. There was some pressure there, and that along with the other injuries, well ... look at it this way, you are one really lucky girl!" She smiled.

"Lucky?" I thought. "I'm real lucky, but somehow I sure don't feel lucky right now. I can't speak right, my thoughts are so fuzzy, and who the hell is Darlene? Wow!"

Then I wondered. "A hole in my head? What on earth does she mean by that?" I couldn't feel anything above my mid section, and I wanted to ask her about that. But, with my limited speech, I couldn't ask anyone about anything. And somehow *'lucky'* just didn't seem to cover any of it! Nothing she said was making any sense of what happened to me. Nothing was clear. So, I let her think that I understood what she was telling me. Then, she said something about a cliff. *'Oh God'!* I don't remember anything beyond five minutes ago. I am so confused.

"Now Darlene, first things first, we are going to wait until you have healed a bit more and then begin therapy." The doctor was taking my temperature as she spoke, and doing all that other stuff that they had obviously been doing every morning of every other day that I had been in this place.

I must have looked blank, because she went on to explain: "We have already talked about this. You are going to begin by going to some classes. They are going to have to refresh you on reading and help you to write. This might take some time in itself. Then, when your body is stronger, you will begin physical therapy. You need to rebuild muscles that have atrophied through your convalescence. They will then teach you how to walk again. All of this is going to take some time, but all of it is necessary for you to be able to move forward on your own."

"I don't know," I said, rather needlessly.

"I understand, that is why you will be in all these various classes," the doctor replied patiently.

"I ... can ... can ... I learn?" I asked.

"There will be a period of adjustment Darlene. No-one can tell you how much you can learn, or how much you will be able to remember. Perhaps everything or perhaps nothing. Injuries of this kind, that is the kind that you have suffered Darlene, well, simply put, nine out of ten people with similar injuries, don't make it. Rarely do we find people who are as determined as you are. In fact, I think that is just what is going to carry you through this. That steel determination of yours."

"OK," I nodded.

I had no idea what I was in for at that time. But in a short while, I figured it out.

But, then, I am jumping the gun if you will pardon the pun. I talked to the doctor, or at least as well as I could, and tried to explain my situation. I told her there were all these people who were keeping a constant vigil over my bed, and it would appear they had been there for weeks now. I was trying to explain to her that I needed to find a way to tell them, that I had no idea who they were.

The doctor told my regular nurse, as it turned out her name was Ginney, everything I had passed on. Ginney in turn, explained to the man and the woman.

"Do you want me to stay here and wait with you until they come in?" Ginney asked one morning.

I nodded to her. *I want to ask them something,* I thought. *Ask them, what?* I tried hard to tell her what I needed to know from them. Ginney looked straight at me and said: "Honey, I do understand. They need to tell you why you are up here in Alaska, right?"

I nodded my head again.

"And they sort of need to fill you in on the past few months, right?"

I nodded again, getting excited at the possibility of finding out anything at this point.

"OK, OK. It's your job not to get too excited. So lay back there and just let things happen?"

I nodded yet again and lay back on the bed. She raised it up a little for me. I should mention here, that I was having a little trouble breathing. You see, somehow my neck got all twisted and distorted when I landed from wherever, and my head was in an odd position. It caused damage I was told to my bronchial tubes and other areas of my breathing system. So, that was the reason they were keeping my bed at a good incline. They didn't want me laying flat. They also explained at the time, that having my bed at this angle just might keep me from having long term problems with my respiratory system.

I coughed a little. The nurse looked at me and asked: "Now, are you going to settle down a little so's I can get some of this information you need? We don't want you having any kind of anxiety attack at this point, now do we?" The caring nurse began straightening the room a little.

Anxiety! I was running on anxiety, how could someone not be anxious when they were sitting in the mess I was in.

I could see I was a grown woman, but I had no idea how old I was. I could see that the man who called himself my father was an older man, so apparently I wasn't a really young woman. I couldn't string a sentence together, much less a paragraph. I couldn't walk, I could barely talk. I couldn't read. I couldn't write. I couldn't do anything a person of my age should be able to do. Anxious ... anxious ... she didn't want me to be anxious. Ha - ha - ha!

When the couple came into the room, Ginney was sitting by my bed. They both hesitated. "Are we coming in too early?" The woman asked politely.

"No, ma'am. If you would both like to sit down, we'll talk a little." Ginney began.

"Is there a problem? Has something gone wrong?" The man asked.

"No ... no ... relax. Everyone should just relax, and let's just talk for a few moments." Ginney took a deep breath and continued, "OK ... OK ... folks. Now see here, the problem is, eh ... mm ... that Darlene here is ... is ... well, her memory is a total blank. There you are now, I've said it. And, she has wanted desperately to ask the two of you, some questions."

She straightened my pillows, and continued talking. "Darlene, as you know, with her injuries, is finding it very difficult to get enough breath to say anything. The doctors have diagnosed, that the part of her brain that was damaged in the ummm ... ummm ... 'fall', was the part that holds most of her memory."

Ginney stopped and looked at me, then the man who would appear to be my daddy, then the woman who would appear to be someone called Nelda. "So, the point is, she doesn't really have a clue where she is, who she is, or how she got here. And slowly, we all have to help her to get up to speed, OK? She might not retain everything you tell her, that's the first thing. So, don't load her down with too much information today, 'cause she's not likely to remember it anyhow, so keep that in mind."

"She don't remember anything, not anything?" The man asked, with a more than surprised tone in his voice.

"No, sir. She doesn't even remember who you are, or why you are here. She also doesn't think she is from here. So, if you could just fill her in on the past few weeks, that would be a tremendous help to her."

I nodded in agreement with a smile. The man started speaking.

"OK, my name is Sam Mason. I am your father. This is Nelda Wright Mason, and she is my new wife. We came up here about three years ago, and we live outside of town

11

here about ten miles or so. Darlene, you came up here to escape Bobby Fulton. He was your husband for about twelve to thirteen years, and from what I gather now, he was a terrible man. Still is, for that matter."

"Married?" I asked. The words came out.

"Yes, you were married to him for that long; you went with him for longer than that. He was a terrible mistake Darlene, and it's a good thing that he is no longer a part of your life. I'm afraid that I'm mostly responsible for you being in that situation, and I'm so ... so sorry. Now after you got up here, you made a lot of friends, had a pretty good job, and met a nice new fellow. And about two months ago, you married him. You all live not too far from here."

"Well," I said. "Children?"

"Oh, no honey," Nelda said. "You can't have kids. Good thing though, considering that horrible first marriage."

I nodded again.

"What else do you need to know today?" Sam asked.

Ginney looked at me, and I said: "Where ... where ... was?"

"Oh, well, you were raised in Murdock, Louisiana. Nice little town not too far from the Arkansas, Texas, Louisiana border. You have a little brother Johnny that you raised. He's a policeman now, in Murdock. He's also a volunteer fireman. He's married, got two kids and another on the way. You two were always very close."

I raised my one eyebrow that was showing beneath my bandages, and shook my head a little. I looked at them, "Don't remember." I said, with a tear starting out down my cheek.

Then I realised that I wasn't even putting words together. I didn't know what was wrong. I was sure that I could at least finish a sentence when I came in here. I'm a grown woman. A shiver ran over me.

The nurse looked at me and must have noticed the shiver and thought that I was having a bad reaction to the information. I must have looked at her much like a deer caught in the headlights of an on coming truck. She immediately began to shoo the two people out the door.

"Ahh, you all need to go now. Darlene needs to rest more than anything right now. The rest of the information can come later. Please, let her rest now and then you all can come back tomorrow." Ginney continued herding them out as she spoke.

The man and woman walked out of the room, and Ginney turned at the door and came back in. She took my hand. "Honey, things are gonna get better for you, I know they will," she squeezed my hand softly.

All I was wondering again was: "Who the hell is Darlene?" Then for some reason the tears started to flow again. I guess it was the shock of awakening to all of this. The man who called himself my dad piled all that information on me and it was swirling around in my head. Then, I realised that the words he had spoken, were slowly falling away as I lay there.

I drifted off to sleep in record time, and then the dreams began.

To begin, I saw a small child sitting in the back of a pickup truck. She was sitting on top of some clothes. I had no idea where the truck was headed, nor did I know who was driving it. There was a much younger version of the man that was in my room earlier today in the driving seat. A woman was on the other side. She had the saddest eyes that I have ever seen, as she looked around at the little girl and the other children in the back of the truck. She was a slight, thin woman who had the look of a person who was on the edge of reality. I had no idea who these people were, or why I was dreaming about them. I felt the wind blowing the little girl's hair, and then I realised that there were two other children in the back of the truck with her.

There was an older girl. She looked a little like the younger girl. I thought I recognised her face, just for an instant, and then the recognition faded away.

There was a young boy about eight or nine there too. He had his hand out, and was letting the wind blow through his fingers as he looked around. He caught something in his hand, and turned and threw it at the other girl. She squealed and knocked it away. It was a large bug of some kind, and they batted it back and forth for a moment. The younger girl screamed with delight watching them taunt each other.

Soon the truck was driving through a small town and stopped at a street sign. The children looked all around at the stores and the people on the street.

The older girl got up and stuck her head through the open back window of the truck, and asked the man driving where they were?

"We are in May, Arkansas. We are going to stay here a while," the man said.

The truck passed on through the small town, and finally arrived at a row of what they used to call 'shotgun' houses. They stopped in front of one of the houses.

The children all piled out of the truck and grabbed whatever they could and began to carry things into the house. It was as if they had done this a million times before.

The scene changed and I could see the two girls walking down the street that ran between the rows of houses. They stopped in to talk to various older people. They seemed to be asking if they needed any kind of help. They appeared to be trying to make money for the family.

Oddly enough, it seemed as though neither of the children minded meeting the neighbours this way. They did finally find some odd jobs to do. The older girl was carrying out trash for some old ladies, and the younger girl was cleaning shelves in a small grocery store down the block. The boy was fixing a bicycle for an older man. So they all did find work.

The older girl called the boy Jack, and he called her Laura. Neither of them called the smaller girl by her name so I couldn't figure out who she was.

The boy Jack seemed to enjoy pulling on the younger girl's braids and making faces at her. He didn't do that to the older girl. I wondered why. His main job, when no-one was looking, seemed to be to follow the little girl around and make fun of her. I suppose that's what older brothers do.

It became night, and the two girls were in the front room of the house and the woman walked into the kitchen and closed the swinging door behind her.

"Oh my. We are going to move again," the older girl said without much enthusiasm.

"Are you sure?" The younger girl asked.

"Yep, when they go in the kitchen and close the door, we are usually on the road again," the boy Jack piped up.

"It's not fair, I have made friends at school already," the older girl grunted. "I don't want to move again so soon." Her words continued through a quivering lip.

"I'm telling you, just as sure as night follows day, we are gonna be piling in to dad's truck and moving to some other place." Jack stated with some authority.

"Well, here we go again," the older girl was now shaking her head as she spoke. "We are gonna pile all our earthly belongings on the back of that old truck, and we are gonna climb into the back beside it. We will then be told to hold some of the stuff down. We'll wave to the neighbours that we barely know, and off we will go to some new place to start all over. I know it. I just know it."

"Yeah, dad will tell mom how great the new place is gonna be, and how happy we are all gonna be. And then for some strange reason they will both laugh, and we will be on our way to who knows where? That's the way it has always been, and I guess that's the way that it always will be." Jack was also shaking his head now as he spoke.

"I don't know. But, I kinda like moving around." The younger girl chipped in.

"That's because you aren't old enough to go to school, and you haven't made any friends like we have. Sure you do. Maybe you are more like them than us." The older girl said with a note of sarcasm in her voice.

"Yeah, or maybe you haven't moved enough in your little life to get sick and tired of it." Jack said.

Sure enough, the next morning the man announced to the three kids that they were pulling up stakes and going to another place. Somewhere called Murdock in Louisiana.

The dream jumped ahead.

The family were now living in a nicer home, a two story house. The older girl was taking the younger two children around, and asking for jobs for them in the neighbourhood.

The older woman, the sad-eyed one, was taking in ironing, and she looked so tired and worn out. She seemed to be standing at the ironing

18

board for hours at a time. She must have gained weight, which made her look a little better.

Then the man told the three kids that there was going to be another child in the family. The older kids groaned loudly.

"Another face to feed. Mother do you think that's wise?" The older girl asked in a tone that shocked both the man and the woman.

The kids brought in their dimes and nickels and quarters and put them all in what was called a 'family jar'. It wasn't a jar at all, but an old coffee can. All of them were working before and after school. The little girl had finally started going to school. She was running errands for two old ladies who lived down the way.

Jack found a really good job mowing lawns for the neighbours and the older girl was baby-sitting all over the town. Everyone in this family was pulling their own weight.

The older girl seemed to be in charge. She appeared to enjoy bossing the other kids around. The parents were the bosses when they were there, but she was quick to take charge when they weren't.

The dream fast forwarded again and it seemed that some years had passed.

The people who were obviously the parents had not gone to the kitchen for a very long time. But, this night, they were sitting in the kitchen talking in hushed tones, and the older girl Laura ran over and listened to what they were saying through the door. Jack watched his sister and just couldn't wait to find out what they were talking about.

"Are they talking about leaving?" he asked impatiently.

"Oh, no. I don't think so. But I don't want to leave here. I've got friends again now. Oh, no, I hate this!" She whined.

"I kind of like the moving around." The smaller girl said again. Both of them looked at her and frowned.

"Well, you go ahead and move with them, I'm staying here!" Laura as it turned out her name was, said with great emphasis.

Laura made a big show out of everything. She begged and pleaded with the mother and the dad, and tried to remind them how happy they all were in Murdock. The adults let them go on for about twenty minutes, and finally the dad interrupted.

"We ain't moving. I've made arrangements to buy a service station."

All of the kids together said. "Buy?"

"Yep. We are gonna see if we can stay here for a while." The dad was obviously feeling very proud of himself.

20

The kids crowded around both of them, and hugged and kissed them in turn. After all, they all had good jobs; the neighbours around them were nice. Laura liked her school, and had made friends with a group of girls who seemed to like her. It didn't appear to matter that their parents were a lot better off than hers. The parents made sure that the kids said their prayers every night, and at the end of this night, they all thanked God for being able to stay in one place for a while.

Jackie and Laura were happy about it, the little girl would have been happy to move. She had gotten so used to moving around, that she rather enjoyed it.

The dad worked long hard hours, and the word around town was, "Take your car to Mason's garage; he does a damned fine job of fixing a car. And he's honest."

The daddy was working twelve hours a day, six days a week. Some of the time Laura and Jack would go down and help him out by pumping gas for the customers, running the register, or cleaning out the repair bays. They enjoyed working together. It seemed to give them all a better sense of togetherness as a family.

The scene again shifted to a churchyard. The man and woman, and the three children were walking toward the church. There was lots' of singing and praising of the Lord coming from the inside. The family joined right in, and were obv-iously long time members.

The sign said 'THE FULL GOSPEL TABE-RNACLE CHURCH' on the outside of the door.

They seemed to be ready to spend the whole day there, as the mother had brought food and put it on a very long table at the front of the church.

After the Sunday service, everyone came out of the church and collected a plate. They filled their plates, with the wonderful southern food on offer.

The children had spent the morning in Bible classes, and then came together in the main bui-lding, and praised God in song. They all listened to the preacher, who was busy giving them a healthy dose of fire and brimstone.

The food looked tremendous, and something that the kids had obviously been looking forward to all morning. There was fried chicken, cream gravy, vegetables, and a whole table full of wonderful desserts. Beautiful cakes, home made pies, cookies, and mouth-watering brownies, all piled high and just waiting for little hands to grab, and gobble down.

The kids played games, and there were races of all sorts. They studied Bible verses and held tournaments to find out which ones could remember the verses best. By the time the child-

ren got home it was very late. They all scrambled to take their baths and lay their clothes out for school the next morning.

The older woman was getting close to her time with the new baby, and one night she was talking quietly to her husband. "The way that women are treated in this church we are going to is worrying me. You see, I heard some of the women talking and whispering. You remember Howard Mull?" She asked.

"Yes," the man replied.

"Well, Howard got tired of Elizabeth being around all the time, and he got the church to dissolve the marriage. It was just like it didn't happen."

"No, I don't believe you." The man was more than surprised.

"It's true. Elizabeth is living in a burned out shack down by the river. She doesn't have any way of making a living, and Howard's got a new wife! That really scares me, it does."

"You are listening to tall tales, they are not true. Some of those old women are just making that up, that's all. They are just stories." The man insisted.

"No I'm not! They were sent away with just the clothes on their backs. All their personal belongings were put out on the porch for members of the church to collect. The church folk took them to some place out of town, in this case down to the river, and left them there. Then, the preacher told Elizabeth, the marriage was over, dissolved, and that was that."

"Nope ... nope ... nope ... It just ain't happenin' that way, no." The man shook his head in disbelief.

"That husband was free to marry anybody in the church. That husband has a guarantee that he won't be condemned to eternal damnation for leaving that woman like that. I don't like that. That ain't right!"

I listened to what was being said, and the kids were listening too, through a crack in the door. The kids looked at each other funny. Like they thought something was going to happen, but they didn't know what.

One day the woman saw a piano on the lawn on a side street, and a woman from their church sat on the front steps of the house crying. The mother didn't ask or hear any part of the story about this woman; she just got more and more frightened about the church. She came in the front door talking to the dad.

"We've got to go to another church." She blurted out. The man looked at her and automatically shook his head.

"Now, you are being silly. No such things ever happen. You are imagining things again.

24

The rest of us are happy in that church. Just settle down, follow the teachings of the church, and stop your silly worryin'." The man returned his eyes to the paper he had been reading.

Seems as though these two argued about everything that was happening. But, now the arguments were getting more and more personal, and the woman was getting more and more depressed as the days' went by.

"Why doesn't he do what suits me, just for once? I can't talk to him anymore without him blowing up." She was saying this over and over, out loud, to no-one in particular.

Suddenly the woman was sad, and did less and less work around the house. She was counting on Laura and the little girl, to do more and more each day. She was relying on them completely to do the cleaning and the cooking.

Since education was free, it was considered a privilege. The mother felt it was her duty to help the kids with their homework. However, she told them, her own schooling was limited, as she had only made it to the eighth grade. This explained why she couldn't help Jack and Laura with the advanced homework they were bringing home now. They were both at Junior High.

She was still helping the little girl with hers, but when she tried to help Laura or Jack, she would break down and run out of the room cry-

25

ing. She was very frustrated with the subjects they were learning, and the more frustrated she became the more difficult it became for her to understand. Finally, she told the dad that he would have to help them, because she hadn't gone that far in her own schooling.

My dream fast-forwarded again.

I could see the woman was getting worse. She was in some kind of deep depression, and the kids didn't know why. They could not understand what was wrong with her. They had no idea what was going on.

In my own mind I wanted to reach out to that poor woman, I wanted to tell her it was all right. But there I was, stuck in a dream with little children, and I couldn't talk to her. I really felt the need to comfort her in some way. I just felt so sorry for her, and it appeared that no-one wanted to help her.

As the years passed, the mother's mental health became worse. She had lapsed into a deep depressive state. She was almost immobile, and unable to cope with daily life.

Soon after that, she began to hate her life, herself, the church, the children, and finally even the dad. Day after day, the mother would burst into tears and run into her bedroom, turn on her fan, and lay on the bed. This happened winter and summer. The noise from the fan would drown out the children's voices. Perhaps if she didn't hear them in her own mind, then she would believe they weren't really there!

In the wintertime she crawled under the feather quilt and lay there for hours and hours on end. She never made a fire to warm the house, or the children. She didn't cook or clean, or do any of the normal daily things that other women did.

I could see the kids walking around freezing cold in the house, but the mother would still be curled up underneath her warm feather quilt. That fan would still be whirling away in her room, full blast.

The kids would run around and holler at her about being cold, but nothing would bring her out of her 'state'. The three of them would begin to call out in the direction of their momma's bedroom, but her private hideaway was not interrupted. It seemed she would go there and completely break down.

If she broke down outside of her hideaway, one of the children would gently take her hand, and walk her slowly back into the bedroom. She started doubting everything, even the things she had said and done. The mother blamed the church for all her troubles.

Those were nightmare days for these children. If the children tried to console her, she would become embarrassed and begin to feel worse. This in turn made her behaviour erratic. The kids were helpless, and when they tried to tell their dad, he would ignore what they said. Perhaps he knew more than they thought, but he didn't offer any help at all.

I thought that more than a bit strange.

He began to tell everyone that her situation was temporary, and that any time now she would get over it, and be better. The more serious her condition became, the more he would try to explain to everyone, the children included, what he thought was wrong with her. He would yell over her loud cries. "It's her time of the month."

That confused the children even more, because they had no idea what her 'time of the month' actually meant. For them her 'time of the month' was every day of the week, as well as every day of the month, in fact it was every day of the year.

Their dad didn't understand, or perhaps he just didn't want to understand, how bad the situation was for the momma now.

Then, it all came to an end one frightening day ...

How clearly this part of my dream was.

The mother had her baby. He was the cutest little boy. The younger girl seemed to pay the most attention to him, and played with him before and after school. She fed him and washed him and kept him clean and nice. The mother seemed to be ambivalent about the new child. But then, one Friday afternoon, when the youngest girl came home from school, I could see her running to the kitchen calendar to see if she had a free hour or two, the coming Saturday. She looked really excited. One of the girls' at school had invited her to a birthday party, and she was bursting at the seams to go.

She suddenly realised it was too quiet in the house, and started wondering what was wrong. The noise of the phone ringing shattered the silence. She ran to answer it, and when she picked up the receiver it was her father's voice speaking. "Where is Jack? He's more than two hours late, that's not like him."

"I'll find him and call you back, dad," the girl replied.

She put down the receiver slowly and turned around. The silence was eerie; she started yelling for her family.

"Momma ... momma ... momma! Where are you momma? Where are you?" She stopped shouting for a minute, and tried to fight back her tears as she listened for a reply. Her words echoed back to her as she ran through the house.

I could see the anguish on her face as she ran. She stopped and looked in each room as she passed. I could see her shivering although it was *warm. She stopped in the kitchen. There was so-mething wrong, and the young girl knew it. She just didn't know what it was.*

I could feel her fear run through me, as it must have ran through her, and I watched her walk out to the back yard. She looked around carefully, then turned and ran back into the house. She stood staring up the stairs for a moment, and then ran up them, taking two at a time.

She called out again to her mother, now ver-ging on hysterics. "Momma ... please, momma ... momma ... please answer me momma, please ... please ... please momma."

Still she heard nothing, not a sound. The em-pty sound of her own voice coming back to her started the tears flowing freely now. She ran to her parents' bedroom and stood looking at the door for a minute. Several thousand thoughts were obviously running through her mind. The fear itself was loud and clear, as her hands were shaking when she reached for the doorknob. A cold hard chill ran over the young girl's body, as she opened the door. It was obvious she was terrified, of what she might find or see. But, there was nothing ... not anything, no momma. She saw only a little note in the middle of the bed. It had her name on the outside.

I couldn't make out the name.

She reached out for it, and then quickly drew her hand back, not sure if she wanted to know what was written on the inside.

She looked around the room, but everything was neatly in its place. She walked over to a closet and opened the door. Then the realisation hit home hard. Her mother's clothes were gone ... gone ... her shoes too. She turned and stared at the piece of paper with her name on it, and reached for it now. She was sobbing openly.

'That's the stationery that momma uses to write her notes on.'

She carefully unfolded the paper, with both her hands trembling. The words written on the inside seemed jumbled and didn't make any sense at first. Then they almost jumped off the paper as she read:

'Dear Darlene and all, I've taken Jack and Laura with me. I'm scared of that church that daddy makes us go to. I'm afraid he is going to turn out like them other men. I got to go, don't know where. I can't live here no more. I know you will take good care of little Johnny. You are the only mother he has ever known.'

Momma

The note was to Darlene, and they say that's me. The note was to me ... me ... and I'm watching my life as a child. This is almost too much to wrap my brain around. How can it be me? I feel my own heart jumping and thumping in my chest; my heart is now pounding like a jackhammer smashing the concrete on a sidewalk.

The young girl sat down on the edge of the bed and read the note again.

Momma had gone; she had taken Jack and Laura and left the little girl alone with her baby brother, and the husband.

I could feel the despair in that child sitting there on the edge of the bed. Her life as she had known it, was completely gone. Her little world had been shattered, utterly and suddenly. Her life now had changed. No more family, no more momma, no more little girls' life. It would never be the same again. Just as if there had been an earthquake, or a horrible burning fire, her family had been ripped from her.

She looked around her. 'What to do? What to do? Oh! God, what to do?'

She was somewhere else now, her little life flashed before her. The church dinners, the travelling, the brothers and sister, the momma, everything she had, was no more. This place, this house, this space in time, was now different. This home, a home where she had felt safe and secure, was no more. Her life ripped out of her little hands, like a piece of paper blown away by the wind into nothingness, yes, nothingness. A little life broken, and carried off by a bird in flight.

Suddenly, the girl jumped up and ran down the hall. She heard her little brother Johnny crying. She had forgotten that her mother's note had said, little Johnny was still there.

His crying voice sounded shrill, almost like a high-pitched screaming animal. She jerked open the door to his room.

He was flat on his back in the middle of his bed, his little arms grabbing at the air, and his entire body shaking with fear. Slowly, he got up as she entered the room, and stood at the end of the bed screaming.

She ran to him and picked him up, she held him to her, close to her, as the child said through his tears. "Momma didn't wock me or wead to me, I scared."

His breathing was erratic, and he was gulping back big sobs. He twisted out of her arms, and the little girl put him down on the floor.

She stared at him for a moment, and then realised that he hadn't had a diaper change for a while. She carefully knelt down beside him and told him that everything would be all right.

33

I could tell she didn't mean it.

"I do love you, my little brother." She sobbed openly. The tears just flooded out as if a dam had burst open. That seemed to be a cue for little Johnny to start crying again. So, she wiped the tears from her face with her sleeve, and told the little boy again, that everything was going to be all right.

Johnny suddenly stopped crying; it was as if someone had just turned a tap off, and he demanded a cookie.

The young girl looked at him saying: "In a minute Johnny, I have to get you changed."

She unfolded a clean diaper and took away the heavy wet one. She powdered him good and proper with the talc at hand. This brought a smile to the small boys face and made him smell a lot better. He put his little fingers out again wanting a cookie. She left him there smiling as she went to the kitchen to look for one. When she handed it to him, his smile widened. The little girl stood staring at him and tried really hard to smile back. The Dad flashed through her thoughts and she remembered she had to call him back, he didn't know what was going on.

I found myself wondering, what on earth could be worse for a young girl than to come home and find out that her mother had just walked out, and closed the door behind her. What *would make a person do that? Why leave two children, why not take them all, or leave them all. It didn't make any sense.*

Like a punch in my gut, I suddenly realised this wasn't a dream I was in at all, it was a horrible nightmare. I felt badly for the young girl. I felt horrible and sad for the whole family.

I woke up. I knew I must have dreamed about something deep in my own sub-conscience. For a second, not more than that, I could remember everything from that dream very sharply. Then, like the pieces from a jigsaw puzzle, the dream started to fade away. I tried very hard to remember it; after all it had just occurred. But try as I might, I just couldn't. Those pesky pieces just kept falling ... falling ... falling ... until they weren't in my mind at all.

How would I ever remember my life? I broke down in tears. I was more alone than I could ever imagine. I was alone, and I knew part of the reason for it, was those images. The images that were locked away some-where, in my mind, but where?

Chapter Two

The Nightmare Continues

I struggled to wake up the next morning. I don't know why. My nurse came in and was ever so cheery. I wasn't feeling that well.

"Hey, what are you so down about Darlene?" Ginney asked, looking straight at me.

"I don't ... don't ... know." I squeezed out, my voice shaking.

"I have something to make you feel better. How about I let you eat some 'real food' today?" Ginney continued.

I could feel myself brighten up. Then I touched my throat, and shrugged my shoulders thinking, 'real food'. I don't know about that, 'real food', food ...

"I'm not sure Ginney, I really don't know if I can eat food, 'real food', as you put it."

"Sure you can Darlene; I know it's been a long time for you, on that old food supplement, but well, it's time to give some 'real food' a try. You will enjoy this, I'm sure you will. How are you about eggs?"

I nodded thinking, 'eggs ... eggs ... eggs. I haven't even thought about an egg, far less eaten one since I woke up. They sound so good. Eggs, with toast and bacon, mmm ... Oh my! I wonder if there will be anything with the eggs.'

Ginney brought in a tray, and there it was before me, a great big soft boiled egg. All I had been given to this point was some water, and that felt so heavenly on my throat. I was really happy with the water, but food ... food ... that was another matter!

She reeled the bed up a bit more, and fluffed my pillows behind me, making sure I was in a comfortable eating position. She handed me a fork and spoon, and told me to watch it, and take little bites at a time. I did. The egg tasted sensational, it was absolutely wonderful. I couldn't believe the delicious taste, I wanted more, I wanted another one.

Ginney creased her brow a little, and frowned, but decided it wouldn't hurt.

An egg! I ate an egg! I was so happy, it was wonderful, it tasted so nice. My throat was scratchy from all the tubes and such, which had been poked down it for some time, but the soft boiled egg, was just what the doctor ordered. So to speak! Anyway, in the end, I had two soft boiled eggs, and a half glass of juice. The juice burned a little, and Ginney decided that perhaps milk would have been better.

Frankly, I could have murdered a cup of coffee. The smell of the fresh coffee brewing down the hall had been bothering me for about a week now, or was it a week, or was it some time now? Maybe a few days, I'm not really sure how long. I looked at Ginney.

"Coffee?" I said.

"Really? Do you feel like a cup of coffee? I'm shocked, but hey, no problem, sure. How do you like it?" Ginney just babbled for a moment.

I shrugged, "I don't know," and as I said it, I burst out laughing. I want coffee, but I don't know how I have it. How ludicrous.

She brought me a plain cup of black coffee; I tasted it, and decided perhaps a little milk and sugar might be a good idea. She had brought that too, so I added a little at a time, until things seemed right. It was good, no, that is an understatement, it was delicious, I loved it.

I had no memory of the dream, or anything that had gone on the day before. Actually, I didn't even remember that anyone had talked to me about my former life.

The man, who was calling himself my father, came in with his wife. They both smiled and sat down in their usual chairs. I smiled back at them, and Ginney cleared away the dishes, and the tray, with the empty egg shells and coffee cup on it.

The man looked at the dishes. "What did you have?" He asked.

"An egg." Ginney answered him automatically. "In fact, she had two of them." Her mouth smiled warmly as she looked in my direction.

"Really, solid food, that's a good thing, right?" He asked.

"Yes, it's a great thing," Ginney replied.

I nodded and smiled. In fact, I found myself doing that a lot this morning. Since I couldn't get my thoughts to my mouth, I decided that perhaps remaining silent was the better way to go.

"Do you have any idea when you will get out of here?" The man asked me.

"No. No-one has told me when."

Ginney shook her head saying. "Mr. Mason, she has a very long way to go, to be cleared for release here. She has to learn to walk, talk, and reason. We have to teach her how to put words into sentences. You have to know that surely. Darlene has to literally start all over again with everything, and that is going to take a while. Unfortunately, adults aren't as easy to teach as children, and that's a fact. So, if she started right now, it would be another three to six months, and the doctor hasn't even cleared her to start yet."

I was absolutely shocked to hear that, and the couple were visibly stunned. I think the man who said he was my dad, obviously thought I would wake up, and be as I was.

How could I be? I had just come out of a coma, and for anyone to expect me to just be my old self, well I ask you? That just wasn't going to happen.

I had survived a fall, equal to falling off the ledge of a twelve-story building, and not a lot of people survive that kind of fall. Modern medical miracles aside, the human body can only take so much. At least that is what my rational mind was telling me.

I also wanted to get out of the hospital; it was no fun here at all, but of course I wanted to be well before I left.

Dad and his *new wife*, (as it turned out), left the room, and I was there by myself. There wasn't much else to do, but nap off and on, until someone else came in to talk to me.

I drifted off again.

The dream came back, only this time the young girl was cleaning the house, and there was a stack of dirty dishes in the sink. The baby was fussing with a toy, and things were not going well.

The young girl wiped her gloved hand across her face and looked at the clock. She picked up the phone and dialed the filling station. "Dad, when will you be home? I was a little late from school, and things are a bit of a mess. I need to put the dinner on, what do you want to eat tonight?"

"I don't know. I can't think about things like that right now Darlene. Just fix what you and Johnny want, and I'll eat something later." The dad hung up.

The little girl stood there staring at the phone and then shook her head. Replacing the receiver, she turned and looked at her little brother. He was crawling around on the rug. He could walk pretty well, she had taught him, and encouraged him to try again when he fell. She wouldn't let him cry, every time he fell. She would just tell him to try again, and again, and again, until he got it right. When he did get it right, she would clap her hands and keep on clapping them. She would make a fuss over him, to let him know how well he had done.

"Dawlin, I want to eat." The little boy said, with the last fall.

Johnny was eating a lot of grown up food now, and her father was making enough money, to buy some of those junior meals that were advertised so much.

She went to the kitchen, and started washing the dishes. She put the washed plates on the drainer side of the sink, and when that side was piled high, she would stop and dry them, and put them away.

In between all that, she had peeled some potatoes and put them on to boil. She was going to mash them up, for part of Johnny's dinner.

She looked up, and there in front of her was a picture of her family, or the family that once was. She stared at it for a moment, and thought. 'I miss my brother and sister. I miss my momma. How could you do this to me momma? Why do I miss you so much, when you don't even want me? You don't want little Johnny either. How could you do this to us? I hate myself for missing you.'

I could feel her anger, she was mad at her momma, her sister, and brother for leaving her alone. She was also mad at her dad, for letting this happen. She was angry at God; yes God, for allowing this whole sorry mess to take place.

The little girl just couldn't understand, or grasp, why any of this had happened to her? She had asked God, over and over again, to please send her momma, and the rest of her family home.

She peeked her head around the corner, and saw little Johnny sitting staring out the window. Then she looked back at the kitchen. She got some meat out of the refrigerator and put it in a warm pan. She finished drying a couple of water glasses and put them on the shelf.

She took a look around the corner again at Johnny; he had fallen asleep, sitting on the couch.

She wanted to cry. She wanted to yell. She wanted to scream, and never stop. She was so mad and frustrated she didn't know what to do. She was turning into an adult woman at the young age of eleven. She had adult responsibilities, and adult time schedules, yet she was a child in school. What was she to do?

Her fear and panic turned to isolation and desperation. She had spoken to her friend Martha Dunsted, and Martha had told her that since her mother had died, her father was taking her out of school. She would be expected to stay at home, full time, and do the housework, and take care of her younger brothers and sisters.

What if that happened to her?

'Why? Why won't someone just tell me why my momma ran off? Why did she take Jack and Laura, and not take me? Did she hate me that much? This is not what should happen to anyone.' The hot tears ran down the little girls face.

'God, please ... please give me the strength to carry on. Please let me be able to take care of everything, and still stay in school. Oh! And could you please send my momma, Jack and Laura back to little Johnny and me?' She prayed earnestly, with clasped hands.

She made an apple pie, and browned it just like her momma did. She woke little Johnny up, and they both walked down to the corner shop, to buy some vanilla ice cream.

"Maybe daddy will feel better tonight. You never know." She said to the little boy as they walked.

Things weren't working out very well. The dad wasn't coming home early, any night of the week now. He would drag in as late as one-o'clock in the morning, and then be gone before she and Johnny arose.

She played with her little brother, changed him, and took great care of him. His daddy only saw him during the day, when he stayed at the station. Darlene was in school for those hours, well, for the time being anyway.

The dad wasn't minding either one of his children. He kept busy at the business, and Sundays were their only day together. He had been too ashamed to go back to their original church, so he and the children were visiting a new church. 'THE BIBLE IS ALIVE CHURCH.'

Sometimes the dad would come home, and help the little girl clean the house.

One evening he came home early. "I want you to know something Darlene. Your momma is very, very ill. She won't be back here for a very long time, well, at least not until she feels better. I know how well you are taking care of things. I want you to know that things are going to continue as they are. I want you to tell me if you are having any problems, time wise I mean. If you need any help taking care of Johnny, or anything else, I want to know. I think that our new schedule is working out well, don't you?" He said finally.

"Yes daddy," she replied. "But who is that guy at the church, that Bobby guy?"

"No-one, honey. Don't pay him any mind." He went into the kitchen to eat his dinner.

She was terrified he was going to tell her that she had to quit school, and take care of the house, like her friend Martha. She took a deep breath and sat down on the couch for a moment. She was so relieved, she almost yelled out. Instead she just took a deep breath and sat down.

The dad was up in Johnny's room now; she could hear him talking to Johnny. He did that a lot these days. He really did want Johnny to know who he was, and even though momma was gone, he reassured Johnny, he would always have a dad.

'Why doesn't he say those things to me?' The little girl was looking at herself in the mirror, as she spoke to no-one.

The next morning the dad took Johnny's hand, and kissed the girl on the top of the head, and said. "We'll see you after school Darlene. Be good honey!"

Everything seemed perfectly normal, except, there was no momma, no Jackie and no Laura in the family, they were gone.

The dad acted like everything was perfect.

Darlene spent the next while wondering, if her dad even loved her momma any more. If he did, why didn't he go and get her, and bring her home? She wondered why he didn't understand, how tough it was on her.

The dad didn't tell her anything, he just expected her to know things, without having to be told. He had no clue, that she was so angry about her mother leaving, and taking her brother and sister. Every time she mentioned her mother, or *spoke about missing her, the father would get angry. If she dared to talk about her sister and brother, he would start saying terrible things about them. So, it was easier for Darlene, to stop talking about them.*

I awoke with a start ... What on earth? Why was I having this dream? I couldn't remember my life before I woke up in this hospital, and yet, in the corner of my mind, lived this dream. I wondered if it was real.

I didn't even know who to ask. I wondered who my mother was.

Was that woman in the dream my mom? Where was she now? Was she still alive? Who knew?

I didn't, not at this moment.

As I sat there looking out of the window at the sunrise, I couldn't help but wonder. 'Will I ever remember? Will things always just come out of the blue like this? Will this dream turn out to be true?'

I reached out for the water jar, and then remembered that my hands didn't work too well. I buzzed for the nurse, and then the dream began to fade.

Those jigsaw pieces began to fall from my memory again.

Chapter Three

My Learning Period

The next five months were filled with hours upon hours of physical therapy and school. This brought tears, screaming and all the trauma that you could possibly imagine.

The lady, who was teaching me to speak again, form sentences, and all that necessary stuff, was a very patient person. Her name was Rosalind Tharpe, and she belongs somewhere in the list of *patron saints*. From the beginning she had a very difficult student and she didn't threaten to kill me, not even once.

I was wheeled into her room on the first day, by my now, good friend and nurse, Ginney Wheeler. Ginney was a hoot! She brightened my days. Every morning when she came into my room, no matter what my mood, (which was often sour), she would crack a joke or just say something silly, or nice. She always cheered me up, no matter what.

Rosalind smiled a little when we came into the room, and I got the feeling that neither one of us knew, exactly what to expect. There was a blackboard, (they are green now), at the front of the small room, and a small desk over to the one side.

We started with a first grade speller, and managed to get through that, in less than a week. Then, it was on with the show. We graduated on to more difficult work, the putting together of sentences, and all of that.

My mood went from sour to bad. I lasted a whole week and a half, before I went into a rage, over a sentence that I couldn't figure out. I was still speaking with so much hesitancy, that I hated to open my mouth. I was so self-conscious about the whole thing. I was trying to say a whole sentence, without taking a half hour, and things were just not working. I just snapped, and roared.

"Forget it." I threw my book half way across the small room. I tried to manipulate the bulky wheelchair out of the door, but without much luck. So much for the dramatic exit.

Ginney heard the commotion and came in to witness my struggle. She just laughed.

That, I must say, was not my finest hour, minute, or time of hospital life.

Ginney's laughing continued for a few minutes, but at the time, it seemed to me like hours. She released the lock on the wheelchair, which I had obviously forgotten about in my rage, and assured me everything would be all right. She pushed the chair out into the corridor saying. "I am taking you back to your room now Darlene, or whereever you would like to go. Just tell me where I can take you that will settle you down."

I began to cry. My crying eventually became a sort of a moan, and to my disdain, Ginney kept on laughing at me. That was absolutely the best medicine I could have had, although I didn't appreciate it at the time. At least I was angry at her, rather than myself for a change.

The studying didn't go as smoothly as I had hoped it would. For the three months I had worked with Rosalind, I kept expecting her to give up on me, but she never did. She hung in there, and eventually, would not allow me to have my anger fits.

The doctor told me, the anger was caused by frustration. It didn't take me long; to realise she was right.

She then informed me, I was ready to begin some physical therapy. This would be on alternate days. Three days a week with Rosalind in class, and three days a week with my new physical instructor, Mark.

"Oh my, something else to get angry about!" I remarked on this new timetable.

Ginney giggled as usual, and the doctor laughed out loud.

Thank goodness, the next day was Sunday. This was the only day I had some time to myself. I was trying hard to remember dad, and what had gone on in my life before waking up in the hospital. I had little flashes of memory. It's very difficult to explain. I still get them, even now.

They are like little parts of a movie, flickering in and out of my mind. Only difference is, I'm the star. I had little flashes of scenes, things, and people. Oh, nothing that I could piece together back then, or even make any sense of, but at least then, I knew there was a Darlene before. I still haven't made her all out yet though!

Dad was coming to the hospital every day. It had to be tiring for him, but he kept coming. I told him he didn't need to come every day, but he came regardless. His new wife came with him now and then. She was very kind to me during that time, regardless of the fact she didn't know me very well.

I still couldn't remember a thing about meeting my dad before. The time before waking up in the hospital was still a complete blank slate. As hard as I tried, whatever was locked away in my memory, was going to stay there a while longer.

When dad came in my room, I had to search my memory to keep remembering who he was. That was a little trying on me, but one of those things I had to get used too.

He would talk about the past, and things that had happened when I was a little girl. I just looked at him, with a blank expression on my face, and he would pat me on the head, and talk about something else for a while.

Finally, I said to him. "Dad, I don't remember any of that stuff. Please, you are just wasting your breath."

"Oh, all right." He would say this, and keep talking.

"Well, there was this boy Darlene. Well, he became a man. We first met him at that new church. Remember?" He looked at me.

"No, dad, that's the problem. I don't remember. Tell me, what was his name?" I asked impatiently.

"Well, one day I decided we were going to change churches Darlene. There were some real nice people at the 'Full Gospel Church.' A young man had noticed how pretty you were, and asked me if he could meet you. I thought this would be a good thing for all of us."

I knew dad was ashamed to face the people from the *old* 'Full Gospel Church', since momma left. But I didn't understand why we were going to this *new* mean 'Gospel Church'.

Dad continued. "You weren't happy Darlene. You showed your disappointment by crying and pouting all the time. You tried everything to change my mind, but I just wouldn't listen. I kept asking you not to sulk.

Our membership in the *new* church was a kind of a curse Darlene. It was there that we met Bobby Fulton. He was not a good-looking guy. He had a big belly, red face, large nose, and curly, blond, reddish hair. But, like a fool, I tried to get you to talk to him, and his family after church. At first you would have none of it, and just went on home.

I knew then Darlene, as I watched from the sidelines, that what your momma had said about the old church was also true about this new one. I saw them trade their wives in for younger women. I also knew some of the men had beaten the wives that they had, and made horrible, disgusting remarks to them, outside of the church. I realised, that the preacher never reprimanded husbands', and he talked down to the women in the church, something awful. But, I guess the thing with your momma, had made me awful bitter. I began to think, that was how all women should be treated, and that's what they deserved.

Maybe things would have worked out better, with your momma and me, if I had been a little more demanding, more of a man, like the preacher said."

I looked at dad. "You really thought that way?"

"Yes, shame to say I did. Anyway here was Bobby Fulton. He liked you, and real soon I started to think that my life would be a lot better, if you kids weren't around." He looked down at his feet.

"I'm sorry for that now Darlene. I didn't know, I really didn't know."

"Well, dad, I'm learning that we can't do much about the past. You know? I mean we can't have do-overs. But, I guess most of us learn from our mistakes, if we can remember them, that is." I sort of smiled.

"There was this one Sunday Darlene, and I remembered this passage, the way it was written in the Bible. I remember the pastor always leaving out the last part, about loving your wife, as you love yourself.

I saw so much in that church, but I didn't pay it any mind. I guess I was really a lot angrier at your momma than I thought."

"Dad, you say you were mad at mom, why was that?"

"Because she left us Darlene, she just took the other kids and walked away. She left you when you were only eleven. That made me so angry, so very, very angry.

I must confess, I was calm when I saw her again, but I was still hurt and angry. I don't even remember what we talked about when she did come." He was looking at the floor, towards the door now.

"So she did leave me? Well, me you and Johnny." I asked, looking for some kind of reassurance. I didn't remember most of my dream, but I did remember that part. I just didn't know how to ask him about it. I took a deep breath, and listened to the rest of his story.

"Anyhow Darlene, let me tell you about the first time you met Bobby Fulton. It's important." He rubbed his index finger across the beard stubble on his chin, and carried on speaking.

"I remember you and me and Johnny, sitting at the back of the church. I was an usher that Sunday at the 'Three Corners Missionary Bible Church.' It was a beautiful sunny morning and this preacher was screaming for all he was worth. The fire and brimstone had been mustered from the soles of his feet, and he was giving it his best. He was ruining a perfectly beautiful day, with his horrible words. Threateningly, he pointed at the women, who in his mind, were guilty of not following *church law*. He demanded those women, 'who knew who they were,' to stand in front of the congregation and confess, or they would be doomed to the fire and flames, of eternal damnation.

The preacher read from a piece of paper: 'Wives submit yourselves unto your husbands', as unto the Lord, for the husband is the head of the wife, as Christ is the head of the church. As the church is subject unto Christ, so let the wives be to their husbands.' He droned on, filling the women with sheer terror, and guilt. This was the preacher's interpretation of the Bible.

He told them, 'as a woman, you have no rights. Never question your husband.'

Do you remember anything about the women in that church Darlene? Dad was looking at me again.

"No dad, I don't remember anything."

"To give you a fuller picture, all of them wore drab dresses that were down to their ankles and up to their chins. The sleeves had to be long, covering their wrists.

They would sit in the church, cowering and frightened. They wore dark coloured ugly scarves, over their long uncut hair. When the minister spoke and waved his hands around, four women jumped up from their seats. With their heads bowed, they ran down the aisle, to the front of the church. They would be prostrate at the feet of the preacher, each of them sobbing, and never lifting their eyes. They were all confessing to the sin of, offending their perfect husbands'. The women sobbed so hard Darlene; you could barely hear them confess.

The preacher would yell out, 'louder you sinner, louder, louder. We can't hear you.'

If you were watching this scene in a movie, you would wonder to yourself, what on earth is wrong with these women? Why would they submit themselves to such treatment? You would also wonder why they don't run away."

Dad stopped speaking.

I couldn't help thinking. 'If you are trapped in a nightmare, caught up in an insane, insidious, threatening situation, all in the name of religion, then you might understand.'

Dad continued. "These women were brainwashed Darlene, they were made to believe that a woman isn't worthy of a man. They believed the teachings of this church and simply followed and obeyed their husbands', without question. They were taught, that women are responsible as wives, to keep their perfect husbands', from the fires of eternal damnation. They were constantly told if they were good, faithful, and pure, blessed and saved women, that God would shine on them, and that was the way it should be. After years of involvement in sick manipulation, and having a thwarted self worth, it became a way of life for the women in the 'Three Corners Bible Church.'

These women thought they deserved the punishment, doled out by their husbands' and the pastor of the church Darlene. They were thankful they had husbands' to obey, and grateful they could help them to reach salvation."

I had a memory flash, as Dad stopped speaking.

I could see these women on the floor of the church, begging for forgiveness, as they swore they would never disobey, or offend any man in their life again.

I could see their swollen faces and bruises around their eyes. I was appalled when I heard what they confessed. One of them said their sin, was not cleaning the house, and watching the devil television.

Another woman had dared to read the newspaper before her husband did. The last, a newly married woman of six months, was severely beaten when her husband saw her application for the cosmetology school. I saw all of this, and yet, by saying nothing, I endorsed the way that these women were being taught. I was there, I was one of them. I did nothing.

"Well, dad, there's this thing about the past, as I said before. We can't do a thing about what we did. We can only change what we are going to do. That's all."

"Yes, I know that Darlene, but what Bobby Fulton did to you, during your marriage, was just dreadful. That's where I'm the guilty one." He was looking at his feet now and shaking his head.

There was an eerie silence for a minute or two.

He lifted his head and looked me straight in the eye saying. "Darlene, I didn't know what I was doing then. And I'm sorry, I'm so ... so ... sorry. You didn't want to have anything to do with Bobby Fulton, but every chance that Bobby got, he waltzed his whole family over to visit us. I allowed that to happen.

They pressured me to bring you back to the church. Bobby assured me it was right for us, and I believed him. He would say, 'his church was God's Church and if we didn't come back immediately, our very souls were in immediate danger of going to the eternal fire.'

He would tell me if I didn't bring my children to the church, I would be destined to hell. He would also say that by keeping you and Johnny away from church, we wouldn't ever be going to Heaven, not even if we died. None of us.

Then every Thursday, Bobby and his sick family, would troop over for more control and madness, and I would let them.

You were just turning thirteen and you were becoming an adult fast. This was pro-bably because you hadn't had a childhood.

Bobby was fifteen. I would throw you and him together on Sundays; he and his family would almost force us to come to that church. I knew that you couldn't stand him, but ... there was something kinda crazy about that whole family. I guess if the truth was known, I was just a little bit scared of them. There I've said it.

Bobby saw you as his wife and told me that he was going to marry you. He tried to push his warped beliefs and teachings of his church, on all of us.

I overheard him tell you one day when he was over at the house, that he wanted you to stop going to school before you turned sixteen. That is what all the girls in that church did. I didn't do anything, and I should have. I should have Darlene.

Don't you remember him saying to you Darlene? He would say, 'Darlene, you must come back to church and bring little Johnny with you. You know your souls are in jeopardy, every day you are not a member of my church.'

Then one day when the whole Fulton bunch were at the house, you stood up and told me, there was no way you were going to marry Bobby Fulton. You went on about having to marry him, and drop out of school. You said you didn't want some pre-arranged marriage, manipulated by some church that you didn't even believe in, and then you ran out of the house.

Bobby ran after you, and grabbed your arm; he threw you to the ground. He kicked you, and stamped on you, and then when I came out, he was standing over you yelling.

'Listen here, you witch, you will marry me whether you like it or not, and you will serve me like the Bible says.'

And then you told him, 'I would rather burn in hell than marry you, Bobby Fulton. And if you ever touch me again, you will be sorry.'

He grabbed you again, and had his hands around your throat, but you kicked him in the crotch, and he fell back. He kept shouting, 'you witch! I will beat you until you behave like a wife.'

Then, I walked out of the house, and grabbed him up from the ground. You went back inside the house crying. You walked through the living room where everybody was, and went to your room. His family got up to leave, and Bobby came in. He told everyone he was going to marry you, no matter what. I didn't know what to think. They were winning me over; I should not have allowed them to do that. I have no idea why I let it happen.

Then, the summer before you went to Junior High, I went back to that church. I would come home and tell you about all the pressure they were putting on me. I believed that I would burn in eternal hell if I didn't go along with them. I know it sounds crazy now, but it was so real at the time. I would almost beg you, saying at the time, 'Darlene, I know you don't want to go to that church with me, but I don't want to split the family. I want us to go to church together.'

You would yell at me, 'I don't like that church. They don't let women have any rights, everything they do is wrong. The church demands women leave school and get married before they are sixteen. Do you agree with that, dad?'

I would reply, 'No, Darlene, I don't. You don't have to follow all the rules. I know you want to go to school and get an after-noon job. You will continue to take care of Johnny too, right?'

I also told you that you would have to follow most of the teachings of the church. I enforced the fact that I was your father and you must obey me. I would tell you if you didn't obey me, I would have to punish you, as Bobby and his family had instructed me.

I was a sick man then Darlene; I was so wrapped up in that church. I believed everything that was said to me. I really thought I was doing the right thing. I invited Bobby and his family over to the house, even though I knew, you didn't like them.

I remember that one day, I sort of smelled Bobby when he walked by. He seemed to avoid baths as often as he avoided school. He started talking to me like I was an old friend, and for some reason I fell for it. He manipulated me, like he did everyone else. I was so hard on you that summer. I think in the end, I tried to scare you, and I could see it was working.

In September, when you started the seventh grade, Johnny was in the first grade. You got up early every morning to cook breakfast, make lunches, and dress Johnny. I would throw my clothes on, and be ready to walk out the door at eight a.m.

Johnny's school was right across the street from yours. You would walk him to his school, and then go across the street to yours.

In the evening, you would reverse the process. You would come home and change your clothes, play with him a little while, inside or out, depending on the weather. You would start dinner, feed us, clean up the kitchen, put my dinner in the warm oven and then you would be in bed about eleven. I didn't realise that you shouldn't be doing all of that. I was so wrapped up in my own thoughts, nothing else mattered.

Some nights I didn't come home until after one in the morning, and you would be asleep. The next morning, it was all to be done over again by you. All your days were the same Darlene; it must have been so hard.

You were growing up too fast. You were a homemaker, a mother to Johnny, and a student. You were always tired. I didn't even realise why, and you seemed to be very distant.

As Johnny grew older, he would help you around the house. You seemed better at the weekends, but then there were those dreaded Sundays'.

There was a new preacher at the church and it seemed like he hated women even more than the other one did. He would read to us from the Bible, and the stories were always about evil women. He never found a good woman in those stories.

He literally yelled the sermon, demoralising women, telling them that they were lucky that men let them live at all. They were worthy only to be servants to the men in their lives.

He would also insist if a woman didn't follow his rules and the laws of his church; or any brother, father, husband, uncle, cousin, nephew or neighbour. Then any man in this church could punish any woman, in a way he felt appropriate.

When I was in the church, I didn't pay much attention to anything else, other than what the minister was saying. I knew you weren't listening, but I thought you were just being mule headed. I knew in some way, that Bobby was beating you, and I knew that was wrong. But in some ways, I thought all women needed a good beating now and again, and I would think about your mother.

Bobby would hit you, and call you a mule. His brothers laughed and egged him on. They told him he had to get rid of any silly notions in your head, about going to school or having women's rights. After all, the minister said the same things, so; I thought it was all right.

Bobby was a horrible young man. He was a bully; he was loud and would embarrass you at every turn. He was not an attractive young man; he was very overweight and used his size to intimidate everyone around him. His whole family were cut out of the same cloth. He told me he would break your spirit, and I wondered if I should have done that in my own marriage.

Funny how things that are so wrong Darlene, can seem so right at the time." Dad was obviously disappointed at his own actions.

"I can't imagine that everything that has happened to me could be your fault Dad. I suppose if I married this man like you say I did, I must have believed what he was saying. I can't help thinking that someone should have stopped him. But, I don't know who, or how they could have."

"Well, listen Darlene, I've got to go. We will talk some more later. OK. And when you think about this Darlene, don't hate me please." He patted me lightly on the head and left the room.

"Think about it? How can I think about it? I can't even remember half of what he said. How can I ever function? How can I go on?"

Chapter Four

A Flash of My Childhood

A couple of weeks later, Ginney wheeled me into my room. I motioned for her to leave me by the window for a while, and she did.

"Now, here you are," she said cheerfully.

She left the room, with a promise that she would be back in a little while.

I sat looking out at the green grass that was beginning to show just a little in the courtyard. There were people walking around and they weren't wearing the heavy coats that I had seen before, so apparently it was warming a little outside.

I could see in the distance a couple of kids playing on swings, and I seemed to blank out. At first, I thought that I was still watching the children playing, but then in my head I could hear them talking as well. I knew that something was happening to me, but I wasn't clear on what it was. I listened closely as the two children talked; I could see the children clearly. They were two little girls in front of me; one was older than the other, and seemed to be more knowledge-able about the subject before them.

Was this a daydream I was having now, or a sleep dream?

"Darlene, Darlene, what are we gonna do about mom?"

The younger girl, who I guess was me, said, "I don't know, Laura. She is all right sometimes. I guess we aren't gonna do nothing. After all, daddy says it is just her time of the month or something. Whatever that means."

"But, Darlene. She's mean to us. She doesn't speak to us for days and she runs into her room all the time crying and such. I don't know. She's been this way since Johnny came. I don't know what to think." Laura said.

"I know. She's awful mean to Jackie. I saw her slap him in the face yesterday. I felt bad for him. But, I was afraid to say anything, cause I knew she would slap me next." Darlene replied.

"Wonder why she's that way to Jackie. She hasn't hit the rest of us yet. Has she hit you Laura?"

"Yes she has, Darlene. You just weren't ar-ound. She's hit me a couple of times, and you just wait. You do something that strikes her wrong and she'll hit you too." Laura looked away as she spoke.

"She's hit you?" Darlene asked wide eyed. "I didn't think ... Gosh!"

"Well, we'd better get home before anything else happens." Laura said, and jumped down off the swing.

The next scene was these same two girls standing next to a house. I seemed to recognise it.

The older girl, Laura, ran to a window and peered inside. I looked at the house. The paint was coming off the side, and the screen door had a huge tear in it. The windows were old and the paint was peeling off them. It was one of those houses that they call a 'shotgun' house. Those were houses that were built straight back. This one had a crumbling cement porch on the front. Most of the houses in this neighbourhood looked about the same, they were all run-down!

The two girls went inside the house. Laura walked over to an old tin coffee can and took the lid off. She put some money inside the can, and then turned and picked up a broom. She began to sweep the tiny, tattered, carpet that was in the middle of the floor of the front room. Darlene went on back to the kitchen and began to clean up the grease and a spill from the morning's cooking. Suddenly, a woman came down the hall. She was yelling.

70

"What are you kids doing, getting home at this time? Don't you know there are things to do around here? Get busy, and I mean right now!"

" But, mom, Darlene has been running errands all day, she made more than five dollars. I have been babysitting Mrs. Donnary's kids. She gave me six dollars, so we brought in more than ten dollars between us, and I'm tired." Laura was annoyed, and she didn't hide it.

The woman frowned and screamed at her some more.

"I don't care what you did. You get yourself in here, and do the sweeping. Darlene get the dinner started. I'm going back to my room." The woman walked away.

"But, momma, we're tired. We need to sit a while, please, can we?" Darlene asked.

"You do what I say. You don't need to be sittin' around here, your father will be home soon, and he needs his dinner. Get busy!" She shouted from the bedroom.

After a while, a man came into the house. I sort of recognised him as the older man that had been in my hospital room. I guessed he was my dad.

"Where's your mother?" He asked Laura.

Laura looked up at him, and pointed back to the bedroom.

"Oh God! Another one of those days. Maybe if we move from here, she will like it more, and that will make her feel better." Dad was concerned and obviously looking for solutions.

"No papa, let's not move. I'm making friends in school, and it's pretty good weather here. I don't want to. Please ... please ... don't make us move again." Laura pleaded.

"Well, I have been looking at a gas station. They tell me it can be bought on what they call 'shares'. That is, I open it, and the guy who owns it will take a percent a month of what I make selling gas, and oil. It's a really good deal." Dad went on to explain.

"Oh papa, please ... please ... don't take it. I don't want to move again. Please, please, I beg you." Laura was crying.

"Well, it's a decision that has to be made by your mother and me, but I'll see what I can do." He smiled and walked towards another room.

Ginney came back into the room and she ran over to where I was sitting.

"Darlene, Darlene! Honey, are you all right?"

I came too, and looked at her pulling myself up a bit, and nodded.

"I was looking." I said, pointing out the window.

"No, honey. You were slumped over the chair, like you had passed out or something. You scared me to death, you did. Let me help you sit up straight." Ginney started pulling my shoulders a little.

"Are you all right?" She asked again, almost shaking me.

I nodded again. "I ... yes, I think so."

Ginney hurried around the room for a moment, and then came over by my chair.

"Honey, are you sure you are all right?" she asked me again.

"Yes, I am. But, eh ... but, but, I had a memory."

"Really? About what, honey?" She asked.

"Childhood, I think."

"Yours?"

"Yes, I have a sister Laura."

"That's what your daddy said the other day Darlene. Apparently, you haven't seen her in a long while though."

"We were children. Murdock, Louis ... Louis ... Louis ... Lou ... Louisiana." I sort of shrugged my shoulders and squinted at her.

"I need to tell the doctor Darlene. Just a minute, let's get her in here." Ginney pressed the call button.

"Yes" a voice said.

"Get Dr Louise Norman to come to Ms. Fulton's room please, 310 west."

"Yes ma'am," the voice replied.

Dr Norman came quickly to my room.

"Is there an emergency?" Dr Norman asked as she looked at both of us

"Sort of. You see, Darlene here has had a memory. She remembered something about her childhood. Now, she hasn't told me all of it. But, it's a start, don't you think?" Ginney explained.

"A memory? You had a memory? Tell me all about it please Darlene." Dr Norman was excited at the good news.

"Well, I have a sister called Laura, and we were kids. Murdock, Louisiana was in it, and I saw my mom. She wasn't, em, wasn't in good shape. She was yelling. I saw my dad when he was young."

"All of that? I am so happy Darlene. Let's do some scans on you, and see what has happened. This is the breakthrough we have been waiting for. Now look, all of this stuff is going to make you relive some parts of your life that you remember. Don't get upset with it. You must keep in mind that you have a great number of physical problems to overcome. So, don't try too hard. Don't tax your body anymore today. We will do some tests in the morning." The doctor had a huge smile on her face as she continued. "I'm just so happy for you."

"I feel very tired doctor." My reply was soft.

"OK Ginney put her to bed and let her rest. Make sure you check on her every half hour today, and the night nurse needs to be instructed to do the same thing. We can't be too careful." Dr Norman turned to leave the room.

"Yes, ma'am." Ginney acknowledged the instruction.

Ginney helped me back into bed, and turned down the lights. I went off to sleep. I felt good. I had a memory. Now, if I could just remember more recent stuff that would be great. 'Well, don't push it Darlene, just don't push it.' My thoughts seemed to be guarding me.

But, I guess once the gates are open, things just come back to you. Slowly but surely I was putting together my childhood. Not the childhood I would have wanted it to be, but the one I owned.

I now remembered I had a brother Jack, a sister Laura, and a dad. How about that?

I took a deep breath, and realised I was tired. I closed my eyes and pulled the covers up to my chin. I must have fallen asleep again.

When I woke up, I tried hard to remember everything I had been told. I tried to put it together with the flashback; I had earlier in the day.

Long shadows were casting themselves over the back of the building, which I could see from my bed. I suddenly realised, I had slept most of the afternoon.

I felt really good when memories came back to me; the memory about the house in Louisiana, and then a little of what dad had told me. And now, I knew for sure, he was my 'dad'.

A thought I had earlier told me, he might have been one of those people who tried to kill me.

It's a funny thing paranoia; how it sets in so quickly when you can't reconcile everything in your mind. Things that people tell you don't seem to make any sense. Your mind jumps immediately to people who have tried to hurt you. Who were they? Why did they want to hurt you? The questions that buzzed around in my head. Yet, I thought sometimes, perhaps I don't really want to know. Maybe some of this is just too painful for me to wrap my mind around. I wished that I could remember everything, and then too, it scared me to think about it.

I wondered a lot, about how I came to be hurt so badly in the first place? No-one had told me. I guess they didn't want to upset me, but then, sometimes the fear of the unknown, is worse than the knowing.

Then I thought, maybe it would be better for me to remember things as they happened to me, rather than trying to remember everything at once.

But, did I have a surprise in store!

Chapter Five

Memories? Not So Much!

The next day, Dr Norman came to my room about 10 a.m. She looked very happy, which rather baffled me. She took my temperature and looked at my bandages, which were finally beginning to reduce. She was still smiling as she asked. "Well, are you ready for your test?"

"What test?" I was surprised.

"The test, the one I told you about yesterday. Just a little brain scan, I want to see if any of the regions in your brain, are showing signs of activity. That's all."

"I ... don't ... em ... I don't remember you saying that I was having a test today."

The smile went off her face, and she said: "What? You don't remember what we were talking about yesterday?"

I shook my head.

"Do you remember anything about your family, and the memory you had Darlene?"

I thought for a moment.

"My dad comes to see me." I pointed to the door.

"Is that all you can remember Darlene? Don't you remember telling me yesterday about your sister, your brother, and your mom?" The doctor asked quickly.

"I was? I don't ... I'm not sure."

"Well, I want to do those tests anyway. Let's go on down, and do the scan. There might be some activity there. I would like to hope there is." The doctor had an optimistic tone in her voice.

I felt terrible. I felt as though somehow I had let her down. I couldn't make up a story to fit what she had asked me. I didn't remember anything about a sister, a brother, or a mom at all.

We went down to the X-ray department. I didn't like this area of the hospital at all. It was a bit scary for me to go into the machine. It's called an imaging machine. You lay in a tunnel, and this red light runs over you several times. This one was open at one end, which made it easier for me to tell them, if I was too uncomfortable. That was a good thing for me, because I don't like tight places and this one was dark, and just made me nervous.

After two hours in the imaging area, I was taken back to my room. Ginney gave me some juice and took me to the sun room. She wheeled me over to the big glass windows, where I could sit and look outside. She sat down on a bench beside me.

"Ginney?" I asked.

"Yes?" She replied.

"Listen, I didn't mean to upset ... em ... you know, you, em ... em ... know who." I gestured towards nowhere in particular, but she had grown to know me very well.

"No, honey. That's all right. We know, you just don't remember, do you?"

I shook my head.

"Don't you worry about it honey. It's gonna come back to you. Just give it some time. The doctor was just real happy because you had recovered a few memories. Well, if you don't remember now. That's just one of those things." Ginney smiled.

I shrugged my shoulders, and was still feeling a bit down. But, I couldn't remember yesterday, much less what the memory was I was supposed to have had. That was obviously, going to be a problem for me.

I couldn't remember dad from one day to the next, and I surely found it difficult to remember Nelda, his new wife.

So, it didn't come as too much of a shock to me, when I couldn't remember what the doctor was looking for.

I was looking out the window when Dr Norman walked over to where Ginney and I were. "Ahh, getting some sun I see."

"Yes, is that OK?" I stammered.

"Certainly Darlene, of course it is. I got some results back from your tests this morning. They have made things very clear as to what your problem is. The good news is, we have two or three ways to help you with this memory loss." She was holding a piece of paper. "Now, this is the problem I think." She was pointing at the piece of paper now. "You see here, where the front of your head was struck by something?"

I nodded, as if I knew what she was talking about.

"Well, that houses your short term memory, and that is the problem. You can see on this scan that there are now electrical impulses, in the memory storage part of your brain. So, this indicates, you may remember things with that part of your brain. What it also shows, is you may only remember them for a little while. So, if you sleep, or think of something else, or there is some other type of interruption, then your short term memory, may not hold on to that former thought. The simplest way to try and help this would be, when you start writing well again, make notes to yourself. Write down something that will bring back that memory, and with practice, you should be able to function just fine."

"What other ways are there?" I asked.

"Let's consider this one first, and see what happens." The doctor replied.

"I've got to go Darlene." She patted my arm and turned to Ginney. "You had better get her back to her own room, she needs some rest. Those tests are very tiring for her."

Ginney did as she was asked, she made no comment.

Later, as I fell asleep, my mind drifted to my lost family again. These dreams were so real, it was just like they were happening that very moment ...

I could see a churchyard, and a church. A lot of people were in front of it. Children were playing around a table that was filled with food. I was a child, playing with some other kids, and we went to the table and filled our plates with nice things to eat. I saw momma there, with my daddy. My sister and brother and baby Johnny were also there.

I was wondering what kind of a church it was, and then the scene switched to the little house that we all lived in.

Momma was telling daddy that the church scared her, and that some of the things they said there, wasn't right.

Daddy was telling her that everything was going to be all right. That no one was going to hurt her.

I couldn't figure that out.

I don't remember much about religion or church; I do believe that I was very involved in the church. I didn't understand why I felt this way, but I just know that I did.

I could hear momma talking again. She sounded very agitated

"Listen to me, those church people. They run some of these women away. They don't like us, I've heard stories. There are stories about women that have run clear off from their homes. They go and live in poverty, on some street or other. That's what happens, if the men consider the women to be unfit as wives or mothers. What kind of a place is that?"

"No, honey, you're listening to some of those old gals' tales again. They don't know anything about anything. This is all just gossip. You aren't to listen to it anymore, you hear me, no more listening to that stuff."

"No, it's not gossip. I know it's the truth. They are ruling those people's lives, and they will do the same thing to us if we're not careful." Momma was not shouting now, she was pleading with dad. She was begging him to please listen to what she was saying, and asking him to please leave the church.

I awoke with the tears running down my face, and I was beginning to get familiar with this scene.

I suppose the fact that my mother had left Johnny and I so young, created a traumatic effect in my mind. I just kept focusing on it. I was reliving the worst experience of my childhood, over and over.

It is a big mistake not to get therapy. Where we lived in the Midwest, therapy was considered to be close to witchcraft. I think a lot of people in the South had the same view. I have no idea where that notion came from. Therapy, or at the very least, counselling, is such a necessary thing. I should have had some sort of counselling, to help me through that traumatic part of my life. But it was never offered, and I suppose, never even considered.

My father was so removed from the entire situation that he couldn't even see, I needed help. Perhaps if he would have told me what a good job I was doing, or made me feel like I was contributing something to the household. Things might have been a bit easier for me, if he had. He never did.

I was destroyed by my momma's departure. I guess that's why the same dream and the same flashes kept coming back to me, over and over again.

Then, without warning, I was quietly sitting on the bed, and a memory began.

I could see myself. It was the strangest thing.

I was running out the back door of this little house, and I ran clear to the back fence. The fence was covered with honeysuckle vines, and I reached for them and covered myself in them. In the darkness, I could feel my entire body shake; tears started to flow down my cheeks and made the front of my dress wet. I couldn't stop crying. I could hear myself say out loud, "why momma? Why don't you love me as much as you love Jack and Laura? I guess you don't love me at all."

No-one answered. The emptiness of the yard, closed in on me, as I heard Ginney trying to wake me up from my dream.

"Come on girl. Wake up! Come on now, come on now," she said gently pushing on my good shoulder.

Finally, I woke up. "What? What is it?" I asked.

"I was worried about you. You were crying again, and making those strange noises. Are you all right?" Ginney was as always, showing her concern.

"Yes, fine, I'm fine. I was just dreaming again. That's all."

"What were you dreaming about this time Darlene?"

I have to think for a moment before I reply. "About momma."

"Your mother? What about her?"

"She left us Ginney." I began to tell her about my momma.

"When?" Ginney was engrossed.

"When I was about eleven, she left with my other brother and sister."

"Why don't you write all of this down Darlene, that way it will be easier for you to remember?" Ginney continued. "Is this the first time that you've thought about her?"

"I don't think so. It all seems like ... ahhh, well, I am sort of sure I've had that dream before but ..." I answered very slowly.

"Yes, so the best thing to do is what the doctor said, write it down. There's no time like the present Darlene, so I'm going to write down what you just told me, and then we'll put it all in a journal for you. That way, it will all be in one place, and you can read it when, and if you want." Ginney was a God-send.

I nodded my approval.

Chapter Six

Will This Nightmare Ever End?

There was some relief in knowing that I could look at the journal that Ginney was creating for me. If my memory wouldn't hold my past, then the book would. It was a terrible feeling not being able to remember things from day to day. Sometimes not even from morning until night. I searched deep into my thoughts to see how I felt about this situation. Then I decided that the journal would have to do - for now.

Normal people with normal memories have no idea what it is like to suddenly discover you have no memory. It has gone. No real memories. No recollection.

If only I could tap into my childhood and see why and how I became the way I am.

I have no real memories at this time, only dreams, and things that others have told me. Can you imagine how exasperating that is, to not be able to fully express yourself? Oh my! I have these really perfect thoughts in my mind, but then, when it comes to having to say them, and to express them to others, I just can't do it.

At this point in my slow and sometimes painful recovery, I still can't make a complete sentence. I still can't complete a thought, to where anyone would understand what I was trying to say.

My mind seemed to be working fairly well, but the memory thing was really bothering me now. I was actually thinking in full sentences, but somewhere between my mind and my mouth, things just weren't coming out right.

Funny how you never imagine yourself, as having any kind of a handicap. You see other people with problems, but it never crosses your mind that, *'there but by the grace of God, go I.'*

"Darlene, you have to be more patient with yourself. You are allowing your own frustration to get in the way of your progress." Dr Norman explained one afternoon.

I nodded as usual. I knew what she was talking about; I just wanted so desperately to get on with whatever life I might have on the outside of this hospital. I also understood that perhaps I was standing in my own way!

"I want to be like you," I said slowly and deliberately.

"A doctor?" She asked.

"No, a real person. I want to be Darlene again. I want to be fixed, and well and how ever I was before I came here."

"I know you do Darlene, and you will feel much better soon. But you have to learn to deal with your own limitations right now, and take things one day at a time, rather than try to bypass certain parts of your progression. I understand more than you know, believe me. Your dad told me you were an accountant, and working for the State Government as an auditor." The doctor sounded very impressed with my achievements.

"I don't remember that." I told her honestly.

"Here are your folks." She glanced towards the door of my room

Dad and Nelda walked in. Dad had a small bouquet of flowers in his hand.

"Something to brighten up your room." Dad said, handing me the flowers.

"Thanks."

Right out of the blue I sneezed, as I took the flowers from his hand.

The doctor looked at me. "Do you have allergies?" She asked.

I shrugged my shoulders. "You know as much as I do."

Everyone laughed, I did too.

Dad took the flowers out of the room, saying as he left. "I forgot you were allergic to flowers. I don't know why I brought them."

"Dad ... the thought ... it's the thought that counts. Thanks." I smiled.

Nelda sat down. "I wonder what he will do with the flowers."

"There are a lot of folks around here that would appreciate them Mr. Mason." We could here the doctor talking to dad in the hall.

"We have some poor souls that never have anyone to visit them. How about one of their rooms?" Dr Norman asked.

We heard dad reply. "Of course Dr Norman, of course."

"Oh! Darlene. Good news. Your brother Johnny is coming up to see you, he should be here tomorrow." Nelda looked a bit nervous as she imparted the news.

"Oh!" I replied. I couldn't remember a thing about Johnny, or any of the other people who had been in my life. This memory thing was really making me crazy now.

"I'm so excited to meet him Darlene. We didn't um ... um ... well. I guess I met your dad, and we headed off up here, before he was even out of High School. Sam tells me that he's a policeman now. I'm real excited, truly I am. He will stay with us while he's here you know." Nelda couldn't help herself looking out the door for dad, she needed her ally.

"Johnny." I asked as soon as she had finished speaking. "There's something ..."

Dr Norman was back, and she and Nelda both stared at me.

"What is it Darlene?" Dr Norman asked.

I shook my head; I couldn't remember what I was going to say. But a memory was trying its best to get through. Again, I was frustrated with myself.

Dad walked back in the room.

"What did you do with the flowers?" Nelda asked.

"There was a lady down the way there. I don't think anyone has been in to see her. She cried when I handed her the flowers. I told her that Darlene wanted her to have them, and she smiled ear to ear."

"Well, you made her day. I bet that is Ms Morris. She's a widow, and her son lives in Oregon. He hasn't been in to see her. I don't guess she has a relative around here. That would really cheer her up Mr. Mason. A big thank you." Dr Norman said proudly.

Dad looked at me as I said. "I remember momma. Why she ... leave us?"

"I don't know why Darlene. She just did honey. I'm sorry, I'm really sorry. I haven't heard from her since her last visit. That would be some years ago now. You were still just a kid, she wasn't well, and finally she didn't have even one good day in her, so she had to get away. I never blamed her Darlene. It was just one of those things that happen. But, how did you know? Are you remembering her?" He asked with some surprise.

"Dreams." I said.

"She had one yesterday and then again today." Dr Norman explained. "But, she doesn't retain them. I think there might be more in the short term memory area, than I thought. But then, at least she is having some memory return."

"Why did she take Jack and Laura?" I asked dad.

"That was a deal we made Darlene. I told her she could take them, and that I wanted to keep little Johnny. She said that Johnny wouldn't stay unless you were there, so, that's sort of how it worked out."

I couldn't believe my ears. "Worked out dad? Worked out?"

"It worked out honey. It worked out. You did a good job; you raised him to be a good man. He's comin' up here on Monday to see you. Do you remember him at all, honey?" Dad was looking straight at me.

I shook my head. "Dad ... I seen him ... when he ... baby ... but ..." I shrugged my shoulders. "In my mind, I saw him. In my mind."

"Oh dear, he will be really sad about that." Dad sounded disappointed.

"Can't help it." I said.

"It will get better Mr. Mason, she is remembering some of her childhood. That is why she asked about her mom. She actually remembered some of the time when her mom was living with you, and you were a family. I have asked her to try and remember things as they happened, this would help her to make sense out of the whole thing. We still don't know if that is going to be possible, or not. But in all her sessions she is being told to remember things as they happened in her life. So far, it's working out that way."

"You mean you remembered your momma leaving us Darlene?" Dad asked as he turned his attention away from the doctor.

"Yes, last night ... wrote it down. Or Ginney did."

"Great! You remembered. Great! Great!" He just kept saying great over and over.

"Dad, I don't remember much now. So, it ... very slow." I said.

"Have you remembered Bobby Fulton yet?" Dad asked.

I shook my head. "Who's that?"

"Your former husband. The reason you are here in Alaska. The reason you are here in this hospital. You were married to him for twelve years, and well, I'm ... not sure you want to remember him." Dad looked at the floor.

"Then." I pointed to my head. "He must be in here somewhere." Everyone laughed.

"It was a terrible thing that I did, honey. I almost insisted that you marry that guy. I even knew that he was hitting you, and I knew that he was hitting Johnny. I should have never left Murdock knowing what I did. I'm so sorry honey! I'm so, so, sorry." His eyes were full.

I shrugged my shoulders.

"Ya see!" He said turning to Nelda.

"Bobby Fulton is, and always was, a really bad man. His family, well, we had heard all about them when we had been in Murdock about six months. His daddy killed his momma, right in front of the kids, three boys. His daddy beat her to death, and is down in the federal prison I hear. Anyhow, their aunt, a mean old biddy named Loretta, took the boys in and raised them. Somehow, every one of those boys turned out to be abusers. Even though, they saw their dad kill their mother, they all beat their wives half to death. And I knew that Nelda, and still ..." Dad put his hands over his face and his shoulders shook. Nelda reached over and patted his arm.

I was shocked, no horrified is the word. I had lived in that life, but for how long? Twelve years dad had said! I couldn't believe it. I wondered why? I didn't have a clue. An abusive relationship. No wonder I had all these injuries. Wait a minute!

"Dad, is this?" I gestured toward my body.

"Well, yes and no." He offered wiping his cheek.

"What?"

"Yes, Bobby Fulton was responsible for you being hurt. And yes, he hurt you all the years you were married to him. But, the two guys that he hired are really responsible."

Dad took in a big breath and continued.

"They threw you off that cliff Darlene."

"Cliff?" I asked, in astonishment.

I guess that sounds a bit strange, but for some reason I had been in this hospital for almost two months, and had never thought to ask what happened to me. I'm not sure that the staff wanted me to know. Or at least no-one, had brought me up to speed. I couldn't get this all straight in my head. I was thrown off a cliff?

"A cliff!" I repeated. "By whom? Where? Why?" I asked.

"Well, there were two guys. Bobby Fulton hired them to kill you." Dad said.

"Are they?" I gestured all around me, panic setting in rapidly. "Here?" My eyes were darting like a deer caught in a headlight.

"No. They are in jail Darlene. See, the funny thing is, they got lost after they left you at the bottom of the cliff. They took a wrong turn or something. Well, in Alaska, it's not a good idea to get lost. There are bears up here that will rip you apart if you disturb them. Apparently they must have interrupted a momma bear's sleep, because they ran back out of the woods right into the arms of a State Trooper. The State Troopers' were looking for them, and so were the Forest Rangers. So, there they were."

"How do they know?" I asked feeling very scared on hearing all of this.

"They confessed. I think, the Forest Ranger suggested that if they didn't tell them everything, they would be happy to take them back to the forest, and leave them with that momma bear. The idea of tackling that bear again, didn't seem to be in their best interest, so they confessed."

"They even confessed that Bobby Fulton had hired them." Nelda added.

"They would have confessed to the Kennedy assassination if someone had asked them. They were not for going back into that forest!" Nelda chuckled, and everyone in the room laughed.

"So, they are in jail?" I asked, just to be sure.

"Yes, they are in jail. Bobby Fulton is in jail, and so are most of his kin."

"When did I meet Bobby?" I asked.

"Darlene, I told you all about that don't you remember?" Dad was getting a little impatient now.

"No dad, I don't. See, that is a large part of my problem. You may have told me all about this Bobby Fulton, but truthfully, I want to remember him myself. I just have to."

"Well, he set his hat for you when he first met you. You were about twelve years old, or so. He introduced you to his brothers as his 'wife to be'. And I don't know, he seemed like a nice boy when we first met. He and his relatives got us to go to their church. Do you remember any of that?"

"No, I don't."

"Well, in a way Darlene, it's not a bad thing. Your life has been such hell, it's no wonder you can't remember anything about it." Dad looked at Nelda, he was struggling to speak.

Nelda rescued him by saying. "God is helping you in that regard Darlene."

She was trying to make me feel like I was being spared or lucky or something.

"I don't know. If I don't remember him, I might go and find another one just like him. Another Bobby Fulton. My God, I will need to remember." I said.

"I suppose that is possible." Dad lifted an eyebrow. "But let's not go through all of that again; let's take it in small doses. That way you don't have so much to remember all at once."

I looked at Dr Norman. She was nodding her head in agreement with dad. "I agree, Mr. Mason."

Then she turned to me. "And you young lady, you need your rest." She looked round the room at everyone. "I think we should give her a while by herself, don't you?"

Everyone got up and started to leave. I was surprised that dad went that easily, but I think that he could see by looking at my face that I was tired.

After they left, it took me a while to relax. I didn't tell anyone, but dad's visits were not the most relaxing thing that could happen. I hated to complain. Dad was trying to do his best. But ... well, what could I do? He was family.

I took some deep breaths like the doctor had shown me, and then I concentrated on the darkness outside the windows. I let my imagination wander, and soon, I fell fast a-sleep.

This time the dream was different. It didn't really tell me anything. I was just floating, sort of like being on a cloud. I could see dad, and then there was this other man. I didn't recognise him straight away, but, somehow deep inside, I knew he was Bobby Fulton. He had to be. He was not very tall, very heavy set, with what I would call 'hammy hands'. Hands that were not creative, not artistic, just short, and fat. He had an extra chin, and hadn't shaved for some time. In short, he was a mess. He frowned at me, and then when I got closer to him, he raised his hand in the air as if to hit me. The look on his face was determined and cold.

Then I woke up!

"So that's who you are?" I shouted out loud.

I wanted a mental image of that guy. I wanted to see him for myself, not have someone else tell me about him. A chill ran down my spine. I think that subconsciously I was remembering more about Bobby than I wanted.

A cold blanket crept over me!

Chapter Seven

The Operation

For the next few weeks my mind was retreating from memory or something like that. Anyway, there were no new dreams, and the things dad had told me were not staying in my mind.

Dr Norman suggested that we stop talking about the past, and consider the future. She wanted to look at what I could do, as far as furthering my own rehabilitation? If I was staying in Alaska, would I be able to support myself? All the practical things.

In a way, I was very happy to be talking about my future, rather than my past. My mind was refusing to consider the past at this point anyway. So, it was time to look forward, to the future, and that was a nice change.

One morning, I was sitting near my window watching the children playing in the park, when there was a little knock on my door. I thought it was one of the nurses' or perhaps Dr Norman, but when I turned to look there stood my younger brother Johnny.

I knew immediately who he was. How could I forget that face? I squealed with happiness and delight, when I saw him standing there. Dad and Nelda had brought him to the hospital. I couldn't have been happier. He ran over to my wheelchair, and gave me a great big hug.

I threw my arms around him and held on for a while.

He drew back a little and asked. "Do you know who I am?"

"Of course, I do, Johnny. I knew you straight away." I smiled up at him.

Dad and Nelda were at the door. "See Johnny, I told you she would know who you were." Dad had a little tear in his eye. He and Nelda walked in and sat down.

Johnny stood back and looked at me. "Darlene, I can't believe you are ... mm ... I mean, well. When dad and Nelda called me and told me what happened, I just wasn't sure ... that you ... Look at you! You look great. How long are you going to be in that chair?" He asked.

"They tell me for a while yet. I'm in rehab and all that, but sometimes it comes very slowly. "

"But Johnny, listen to her. She is making full sentences now. She's so much better than before. She has made great progress. Nelda and I are so pleased." Dad finished.

"I still have trouble remembering all the words though, but, all in all, I guess I'm ahh, doing all right."

"Great, just great Darlene." Johnny crossed the room to pick up a chair.

"When did you ... ahh?" I tried to ask.

"Get here?" Johnny finished my sentence for me. "Just this morning. Dad and Nelda picked me up from the airport. Listen Darlene, Bobby Fulton is in jail. I'm not sure whether you will be pleased about that, or not. But, he's on death row."

"What?" I asked.

"He killed a policeman. He tried to escape about six months ago. He managed to get a gun from somewhere. When the police closed in on him, he tried to shoot his way out. They caught him, but not before he shot a cop. The court trial didn't take too long this time, and he's been on death row now for about four or five months. He's supposed to be executed next year." Johnny said.

"That long?" Dad snubbed.

"Well, yeah. He has some appeal time left apparently." Johnny answered.

104

"For him, there should be no appeal time." Dad growled.

"Dad! There should be time for everyone." I am not sure why I said that.

"Even him Darlene?" Dad looked at me in astonishment.

I nodded yes.

"Well, I don't agree Darlene." Dad was obviously annoyed.

"Come on guys. Let's talk about something more interesting than Bobby Fulton," Nelda asked diplomatically.

"Yeh, Nelda is right Darlene. Where do you want to go when you get out of here?" Johnny asked.

"I hadn't thought that far ahead Johnny." I was being honest with him.

"Besides, there's this fellow that she's not telling you about Johnny." Nelda lifted one eye.

"Fellow? What fellow? A new fellow?" Johnny was intrigued.

"His name is Jerry. He worked with me at the office; he's only been to see me a couple times." My face flushed.

"I don't know about that." Dad raised an eye, as Nelda had.

"He wants her to move to Florida with him." Nelda chipped in.

"That's an interesting thought. I think, if I were you, Darlene, I might consider that move. Brrrr, I'm not a big fan of Alaska." Johnny laughed and rubbed his arms. "Too cold up here, don't you think?"

I nodded my head and smiled.

Johnny stayed for three more days, and then he had to go home. He had married, and his new wife was expecting their first baby. She was due any time now, and he needed to be with her. He was working as a policeman now, having moved from the Fire Department. He seemed to like his new job and the freedom it brought with it. He seemed to be making a little more money which would help with the baby coming.

Funny, while Johnny was visiting me, my memories of him, and our early times together came flooding back. I didn't have to be asleep, or dreaming to remember him. I remembered him as a baby, a child, and now a man.

I also remembered when dad insisted that I marry Bobby Fulton.

I was about twenty years old, and I sort of remember being in classes. I suppose, that was when I was taking the medical courses at the Junior College. Then, I remembered talking to dad about using my medical training, perhaps moving to another town, a larger town, and getting a really good job. Dad more or less, flew in to a rage, I remember him arguing with me.

"That's not a good idea Darlene." He was more than angry as he shouted.

"I don't know why daddy, I could get a good job, and take Johnny with me. He could finish school, and we could have a better life, if I made more money and ..."

"Darlene, you are going to marry Bobby Fulton. All our friends at the church think it's a good idea, and so do I. So, that's final. You can take Johnny with you. Bobby has already agreed to that. Bobby is going to get a church of his own. He will be the minister, and you will be his wife. And that's that." Dad stormed out of the room.

I remember being reduced to tears. I couldn't imagine why my daddy would even consider me marrying that man. I didn't like Bobby. He was coarse, and hard headed. He had hit me before. Dad had told me about Bobby's own father actually beating their mother to death. He did it right in front of the boys' eyes. My dad knew that. Bobby would hit me, I knew he would. He would curse me out, and be ugly to me. I couldn't imagine why my own father would sell me out like this.

I remembered long nights of worry, and wondering why on earth I had to go through this horror.

Then the fateful day came.

I sort of remember the wedding. Bobby showed up in his faded blue jeans and a suit coat that was too big for him. His brothers all lined up behind him, all of them in blue jeans too. The little church was too hot to breathe in. All those people, good members of the church turned out to see the wedding.

The women with their long skirts, and long sleeves down to their wrists. The high necks on their dark, ugly dresses, and their long, unmanageable hair, piled high on top of their heads. They wore no makeup. Half of them sat there, with bruises and cuts all over them. Their recent beatings evident, for all to see. A gift from a husband, in payment for some minor transgression.

The men sat on the other side of the church, with their Sunday, 'go to meeting' clothes on. They sat in a very imperial way. That was the way the church believed they should sit. Men were the absolute rulers of the house, and of the wife. The wives were nothing more than mistresses and housemaids to these men. If they got out of line, the men were allowed, no required, to beat them into submission. If this didn't make the women become 'good church women', the church would help the men to get a divorce.

These wretched witches would be more trouble than they were worth. The church would then help the men to find 'good' women members of the church, who would submit to their every whim.

I remember very little else. The wedding was over, and I don't even remember what I was wearing. A suit, I think. I remember being whisked off to a tiny, dirty little motel, and having my clothes ripped off. I remember Bobby Fulton crawling on top of me, to do his business. I also remember him rolling off me, and him falling fast asleep. I remember very well, how dirty I felt. I tried to shower and get the feel of him, off my body, but somehow I couldn't get rid of it.

I race ahead with my memories, and I remember Bobby locking me in a closet, because I had misbehaved. I also remember Johnny coming home from school, to find me still locked in a closet. I remember Johnny, and some other children, getting me out of the darkness, and Bobby coming in and finding me free. Bobby started cursing and yelling, and beating Johnny so badly, that I had to take him to the emergency room. I remember the doctor telling me that Johnny had several broken bones.

Then I remember Bobby being in jail for beating Johnny. Johnny was only fifteen at the time.

I remembered Johnny had to go and live with a doctor, because Bobby might kill him, if he came back and lived with us.

I think I worked for the doctor, or somehow knew him. Johnny stayed with the doctor and his wife until he was eighteen, he never moved back in with us.

I told Johnny about all these memories.

"That's good sis. I think it's good that you are remembering everything. Don't try too hard. It might be too much of a strain on you." He cautioned with concern.

I nodded my head and told him. "Dr Norman said the same thing Johnny. She told me that remembering too much at once, could sort of overload my circuits."

He laughed out loud.

"But, Johnny, I want to remember. I feel so ... so ... I don't know how to say it, but it's just so hard. It's just unbearable sometimes, to have no memories at all."

"Darlene, perhaps it's just as well. You have enough to deal with while you are recovering physically."

"Why would you say that Johnny? Dad said the same thing."

"Darlene, things were bad between you and Bobby. He treated you awful. He beat you and he ... he ... well, never mind, he just did all kinds of terrible things. And ... and, it's just better that you don't remember all about it. You are in enough pain physically without being in pain mentally as well."

His voice held compassion and sadness. It made me wonder, just how bad was it?

"I guess you're right Johnny." I shrugged my shoulders, as usual.

"Listen, I've got to go sis. I told Delores I'd be back today; I've got a plane to catch. I hate to leave you, but, I'll try and get back up, just as soon as I can. Listen, you take care now, and know that I love you." He bent over and kissed me on the cheek.

I was so glad to see him, and so glad to get more of my memory back. I knew from listening to everyone, that many of my memories weren't going to be good ones, but at least they would belong to me. I preferred the memories, as opposed to something that someone had told me.

I really hated to see Johnny go, but I knew his new family had to be his priority. He walked to the door, and turned to give me a last look. He smiled his silly little smile and walked out the room. I smiled to myself as he left. A huge feeling of pride swept over me, as I realised this handsome, kind, guy, was my brother. Of course I'm just a little prejudice!

Dad popped his head round the door as Johnny left. "You all right today, Darlene? I'm rushing to take Johnny to the airport."

"Yeah, fine Dad. I guess so. I hate to see Johnny go. You all drive careful now." A sadness came over me like a cold cloth, and Johnny was gone.

I told Dr Norman about all my memories, and she seemed pleased. I told her I was remembering my ex-husband, and a little of our life together. A little frown crept over her brow at the mention of my ex.

"Don't remember too much about him. He doesn't seem to be worth it!" There was quite definitely a note of disgust in her voice.

I shrugged my shoulders. "You know what Dr Norman; I don't think he's worth it either."

"Listen Darlene, about these memories. You say they came back to you while you were awake this time?" Dr Norman asked politely.

"Yes, I could remember as I talked to my brother."

"That's good. That's really good. But, we need to be careful. Memories might come flooding back at any time now. You have to be sort of prepared to remember and process them Darlene. You do this quickly, and then move on, and concentrate on whatever you were doing, before the memory came. OK?"

"OK." I replied

I wondered what she really meant by that. At this point I didn't have to worry anyway, as yet again, for the time being anyhow, my memory powers had left me. And perhaps everyone was right; it may have been a good thing, after all.

The only good thing about my lack of memory at this time was I didn't have any thoughts about my ex-husband. I had no idea at the time, what I had lived through, other than my incident with the cliff.

I have to agree with the doctor, it was a good thing that I couldn't remember my life with Bobby. Twelve long years of trying to do the right thing, of trying to make a marriage work, and twelve long years of living in hell.

The next few weeks were filled with intensive therapy, both mental and physical. The doctor agreed it was time I got on with my real life, and she was working with the physical therapist, to make me stronger and more self reliant. They did a great job; I became able to stand on my own.

Now if I could just get that writing thing down a little better ...

Chapter Eight

Jerry Comes To Call

I continued to recover; dad and Nelda were amazed at the speed of my physical recovery. I could now dress myself, and get out of those terrible hospital clothes. Every week, I spent more and more time away from my wheelchair. I was now relying on canes to steady myself as I walked.

The doctor's only concern now was my memory. That process seemed to be a lot slower. I had remembered a great deal of my life before the cliff. That wasn't the problem. I just wasn't retaining a great deal of what I was being taught. Dr Norman looked concerned every time she visited me.

Finally one day, I plucked up the courage to voice my opinion. "Look doctor, the thing is, I'm going to have to figure a lot of this stuff out for myself."

"I know that Darlene, but I was hoping your memory retention would be a lot better before you were released."

I was in shock at her statement. "Doc ... doc ... I don't understand, released? You have never mentioned re ... re ... re ... release before, we never ever talked about that, no, not ever."

"I know Darlene. But it is the time now to think about your going home. We can finish some of your rehab as an outpatient. We also have to consider now, what you are going to do with the rest of your life. You are a young, vibrant woman. I have noticed your friend Jerry has been visiting you a lot recently. Is there something in it? Is he more than a friend?"

"Jerry wants to marry me doctor. And I haven't answered him yet. I couldn't tell him when I was getting out of here. All of these questions, and no answers. You know what I mean?"

"Well, that answers one of my questions, but are you going to marry him? I mean, once you are released Darlene?"

"I'm not sure. I mean, my other marriage didn't turn out so good, did it? I, em ... em."

"Darlene, I think you should consider speaking to a counsellor, or perhaps the staff psychologist. After all, everything you have told me about your married life before you were thrown off the cliff, is a horror story. I

116

think some counselling, would help you deal with some very important issues."

"Oh, truthfully doctor, counselling is out of the question for me. I have worked with everyone here, and I feel that I have left everything behind me. I think I'm fine to go on with my life."

"I really do recommend counselling Darlene, I was thinking along the lines of abuse counselling, and perhaps, long term. When you consider the fact that you were living in an abusive situation for all those years, you need someone to help you deal with all of that. It may also help you with the rebuilding of your new life."

"Really doctor, I appreciate your concern but I think I've got a handle on it. I have seen so many doctors and nurses'. I mean, I know you mean well, and you might be right. But I just don't want to go down that road right now."

"Darlene, you are a very bright young woman, but I feel I must say, in my opinion, this could be a mistake." She started toward the door.

She looked back. "But, it's your mistake to make, I guess. We'll talk later."

I thought about what she said, I really did think about it, and did consider her point of view. But psychiatry, I mean to say, psychiatry, well that was just something that was never ever talked about in my family. I always thought there was something sinful about dealing with a psychiatrist. That was a huge mistake on my part.

I had remembered almost all of my life at this point. I remembered marrying Bobby, and the horrible existence that we lived. I remembered all the beatings and the verbal abuse he dished out to me, on a daily basis. And I remembered something else.

I was sitting in my room in that horrible wheelchair, and staring out my window again. I had this real strange memory flash.

It was the summer before my senior year. I had made plans for my future, dressed real pretty, and felt I was mature enough to work full-time. This would allow me to save some money for college. I took Johnny over to the city park to play everyday. He learned to swim, play baseball, and get along with other children. I missed Laura and Jackie terribly. But dad never mentioned them.

It was summertime, right after school was out, and momma made one of her visits with my sister Laura, and brother Jackie. We lived in Murdock at the time.

She would go straight to her friend Betty James' house. She would then bring my brother and sister to our house to visit us, it was really weird.

It was like they were strangers to us. We were all strangers to each other. Laura and Jackie were allowed to stay overnight with us, but we had very little to say to each other, we would get bored and go to sleep.

Laura snored loudly. It was so annoying I had to put a pillow over my head, to try and block out the sound.

When morning came, they would be gone. They were never there when I got up for school. Dad never got to see Laura and Jackie, and complained bitterly if we didn't call the station to let him know they were visiting.

Momma said she would prefer, if we didn't call him.

I didn't want to upset her by calling him; she seemed so nervous and still cried about everything. I always hoped she might go to the station and see him. Betty could have driven her, but she didn't offer. Laura and Jackie wanted to visit their old friends, so they didn't spend much time with Johnny and me. I told Laura about my job at the doctor's office. Her attitude was, so what. I think she was jealous; she certainly acted like she was. I would keep quiet and let her brag about her own wonderful life in California.

I would pick Johnny up after work and take him home quickly to let him spend a half hour with Laura and Jackie, before he went to bed.

Momma always told them, they would leave early in the morning. When Laura and Jackie were there, Johnny didn't know either one of them. Johnny was a baby when they left, and when they returned, they were like strangers in our home. It was very awkward, and sad at the same time.

We were all children of the same family, but I knew more about my neighbours than I did about my own family. They were odd to me. We just couldn't communicate.

Johnny loved telling me all about his day and he would use all the sounds and gestures. I would tell him about my day too. We were very close Johnny and I, almost like mother and son.

I cut my hair. It was so comfortable. I started going to church with dad, mainly to keep the peace. He liked me sitting next to him in the church. When church was over, I would go straight home. I didn't see Bobby for a week or two. Thank God.

But then, when I went to drop Johnny at school in September, I saw Bobby standing in front of the building. I ran around to the back and was going to hide until he left. I knew the doctor would understand if I was late for work. I had told him some of the cruel things Bobby had done to me.

The church demanded that women do not cut their hair, so I wore a hat on Sundays'. But this wasn't Sunday so I didn't have my hat on.

I thought I heard footsteps and ran around to the other side of the school. I came face to face with Bobby. He had an evil look on his face, and I knew that meant trouble.

He grabbed me by my hair and threw me to the ground, holding my mouth shut with his hand. He elbowed me in the stomach and dragged me to the back of the school. He kicked me again and swore at me. He dragged me over the stones which hurt my back and bum. He was yelling about my hair. I could see Johnny running towards me, I was hoping he would stop. I didn't want him to get hurt.

Bobby pulled me over to the swing, kicking me in the back. Johnny kept coming, and jumped on Bobby's back, trying to hit him in the face. Bobby threw him off with such force, I was afraid he had broken Johnny's back. He struck me with his fist, smashing my teeth. I could taste salty blood.

"No wife of mine is ever going to cut her hair. You hear me? You already break our rules by working, and now this, you know this is against our church beliefs."

He threw me to the ground like a rag doll, and kicked me in the head and neck. I winced in pain and curled up to protect myself from further blows.

"If you ever cut your hair again, I will kill you, you witch. You hear me? You listen good bitch? I will kill you."

I had to stay away from him. I wasn't going to that church again. If dad wouldn't listen to reason, I planned on running away and taking Johnny with me.

That night, I told dad exactly what happened to Johnny and me. I also told him, I was never going to set foot in that church ever again. I turned his face to look at me. "Do you hear me dad, do you understand?"

"We'll see, Darlene, we'll see."

"No, we won't see dad. I mean it this time, never again."

My senior year was exciting, full of activities with the girls, working after school and doing my nightly chores. I didn't go to church. Johnny went with dad and sat in the front pew.

With the increasing visits from the church-women, dad weakened again.

"You must go back Darlene. They come every night. I can't stand it. Please go back, will you Darlene, please?"

I saw the desperation in his eyes.

"I will go back, but only if you promise me, I can attend vocational school after graduation. If you don't promise me that, I'm moving out of the house, and taking Johnny with me."

Dad paced the floor and said he didn't like me talking to him like that.

"We'll see, we'll see, Darlene."

I stopped him.

"Please don't say that to me again dad. We will not see, it is a straightforward, yes or no!"

Dad raised his hand to hit me, but Johnny came into the room. Dad dropped his hand.

"Yes, if that is what you want. You may go to school, but please don't leave the house Darlene." Dad lowered his voice in defeat.

I thought dad's decision to let me go to school, and attend church once a month would make my life easier, but I was wrong. The church women shunned me, talked against me, pointed at me on the street, and laughed at me. They called me names like Jezebel, whore, harlot, and bride of Satan. They always spoke loud enough for other people to hear them.

I tried to ignore these women. I would hurry through the grocery store and grab my bags quickly and get out. They wouldn't stop. One of these women would call me on the phone; she would call me one of their pet names, and then hang up. My Dad knew about all of this harassment, but he didn't say a word.

Finally, one beautiful September morning, I graduated and entered the School of Nursing. It was just as I had planned. By this time, I was working for the Doctor only part time, and my little brother Johnny was growing tall and independent. He had just turned thirteen years old. How time was flying.

Bobby walked behind me at the orientation on my first day of Nursing School. I tried to mingle with the other students, tried not to act scared. I didn't talk to Bobby. He circled me like a lion trapping his prey. I was terrified, but everyone was laughing, talking, not paying any attention to us. He shook his fist in my face and whispered: "OK you witch! You finish school, but when you graduate next year, you are going to marry me. You hear? Otherwise, you will live to regret it."

He started to slap me, but I blocked his fist with a book, and clouted him so hard on his head that I drew blood.

I planned on graduating, getting a job in another city, and taking Johnny with me to make a new life. I wanted to be as far away from Bobby

Fulton, and his crazy family, and his sick church,
as I could possibly get.

I was jolted back to my own reality when someone dropped a food tray in the kitchen. When I realised where I was, I also realised I was in a cold sweat, and my hands were shaking uncontrollably. I was trembling, and the sweat was running down my back. My nurse Ginney came in. She took one look at me. "My God girl. What is wrong with you?"

"No, nothing Ginney. I just ... had ... had ... a memory."

She stared at me. "Darlene, this is a problem. You have got to stop thinking so much. You are going to have some sort of an episode if you don't. The doctor didn't go into it much with you, but she wasn't kidding when she said; don't dwell on the past too much. She's afraid that if the memories come flooding back too soon, that you might, well let's just say that it could cause a lot of damage, perhaps a stroke. So please, start thinking about your future for a change, and leave the past where it belongs."

"I didn't know that Ginney."

She walked over to fluff my pillows and stared at me.

"Look Darlene, are you thinking about that lousy ex-husband of yours?"

I nodded yes.

"Well, stop it! Stop it now. What part of that do you not understand?" Ginney was a gift from God.

We both laughed at her scolding me like a child.

Later that day I had another memory.

I remembered that I worked for a doctor in Murdock, Louisiana. While I was there, I learned a lot more about my ex-husband than I wanted to know. I have no idea why I remembered this one incident in the doctor's office, but I did.

It all came flooding back.

There was a patient there; her name was Price I think.

Anyway, I remember sitting at my desk one day when Mrs. Price came into the office.

"I have to see the doctor," she said, in an urgent voice.

"He's with a patient right now Mrs. Price. Is there something that I might do for you?" I asked politely.

"No dear. I must talk to the doctor, right away."

"He should be finished with ... oh ... look he's coming right now."

126

The Doctor walked to my desk and I leaned toward him, speaking in a low voice. "Doctor, Mrs. Price needs to see you real bad." He looked at Mrs. Price and then me.

Mrs. Price had a look on her face that you don't see very often. It was one of horror and anger, somehow mixed together in a weird way.

The doctor motioned for her to come inside his office.

Even though they closed the door, I could hear their voices, and what I heard shocked me to the core.

"Doctor, Marybelle is pregnant, four months gone, and she says that Reverend Fulton is the father of the child. I don't know what to do; I just don't know what to do." Mrs. Price was crying.

"Pregnant? Marybelle? Are you sure? Why didn't you bring her in? Oh, four months, you do realise it's too late to do anything about it, don't you?" The doctor was sympathetic.

"Oh, we wouldn't ever have considered an abortion anyway doctor. We don't believe in that sort of thing." Mrs. Price composed herself.

"I understand that Mrs. Price, but you also have to understand that your daughter is only thirteen years old, and that this pregnancy could ruin her life. The chances of the child being normal are not good. Besides messing up her hormonal balance, and doing great harm to her

reproductive system, her own system is not yet matured, and certainly not enough to ... to ... bear children. Furthermore, she will need a great deal of counselling as well." The Doctor finished.

"We know all that. Marybelle is going to live with my sister in another town. My sister is going to care for her, when the child is born, it will be put up for adoption, and then Marybelle will come home, and finish school. That's what's best for all of us." Mrs. Price had obviously thought this through.

"Well, I should still like to check her over just to make sure that everything is all right with her, physically."

"Let me come to your house, Mrs. Price. You do know that my secretary is Reverend Fulton's wife, don't you?"

I couldn't hear what she said. But then the Doctor said. "This is going to be a very embarrassing situation for all of us."

I walked out the door of the doctor's office in a state of total shock and disbelief. For a moment I remember not being able to get my breath. After all the things I had put up with, trying to make my marriage work. All the beatings, the shouting, the cursing. Now this! He was having sex with a child. Worse than that, he had gotten this same child pregnant! I couldn't believe it, but then I remembered little things. Little indicators

128

that he was being unfaithful. They always say the wife is the last to know, when in truth, she is the first to know, but the last to admit it.

He had been less interested in having sex with me, and he was staying away from the house a lot more than he had in the past. I should have known. There were glances, between him and someone in the congregation, I just had no idea that it was between him and a child.

I remember walking in the front door of our run-down little house. Bobby was there, sitting in his chair and drinking beer. I looked at him for a moment and smiled. This was rewarded by him yelling.

"What are you doing home in the middle of the day Darlene? God! Don't tell me you were fired. We can't afford for you to be fired."

I continued to smile, and he stared back at me.

"All right Darlene. What is it, what is wrong with you?" He asked.

"I know what you've been doing Bobby Fulton, and in fact, I know who you've been doing it with!" I hissed the words at him through clenched teeth.

"What the hell are you talking about?" He started to get up from his chair.

"Marybelle Price is who I'm talking about. The name sound familiar?" I stood my ground.

He looked stunned for a moment, and then the blood rose to his face, slowly turning it bright red. The veins in his neck filled up, and looked as though they were about to burst.

"That's a damned lie! I ... she ... she's just a kid. What kind of lies are you spreading? You had better ..."

I didn't let him finish his sentence. "Sit down, the girl is pregnant with your child."

"That's not possible. I never touched her, I never touched that kid." He yelled.

"Well, Marybelle told her mother you did, and her mother believes her. I believe her too, and so do the police, they will be coming here just shortly." I walked around him enjoying every minute.

"The cops! What do you ... did you call them? I'm sure you did, you fucking bitch! You'd do anything to get rid of me, wouldn't you?"

From what I remember, it wasn't too long before the police arrived and cuffed Bobby. They took him to jail for molesting a minor. I was in shock, but glad at the same time.

Unfortunately, some of the church members who didn't believe a word of the charge, got him out in a few days. But I enjoyed my short vacation from him anyway. Or so I thought.

My nurse and friend Ginney walked into the room, and I told her all about my new

130

memory. She quickly wrote it down, as she had done with all the others.

"There's something else Ginney, other than the memory I've just told you about. I want to ask you something. Did I have a full hysterectomy? I have a scar. I think I had some kind of emergency, did I?"

"Yes, we sent for your records some time ago and they said that you had endometriosis. Apparently, you had an event in a Doctor Chase's office. You were rushed to hospital and emergency surgery was carried out. It must have been very painful for you." Ginney's face expressed sadness.

"I suppose it must have been painful. But the end of that story is, that I can't have any kids Ginney, is that right?"

"No, that's not right Darlene. Well it is and it isn't. There are so many other ways you can have children nowadays. There are lots of couples now that aren't having kids. I suppose it sounds a bit selfish, but Charlie and I have decided not to have any kids."

"You don't have any children Ginney? I thought you did. You would make a great mother. Why did you decide not to have kids? Not that it is any of my business of course."

"It's OK Darlene, I don't mind you asking. We decided that with the world being as it is today, and the trouble that kids can get into, well ... you know what I mean. It just seems too much of a risk. And my Charlie is a bit of a big kid himself, and if I'm honest, I am too sometimes. So we decided it was the best thing for both of us."

"But Ginney, what if something happens to Charlie? You will be all alone."

"We both thought about that, but we decided that we would either find someone else, or live by ourselves. I didn't get married until a few years ago; Charlie and I were older single people. With my work I didn't have time to find a husband. And Charlie had gone with several women, but never found one that he wanted to marry. We had both almost given up the idea of marrying when we found each other, and we enjoy our freedom. We throw the dogs in the back of the car, and go anywhere we want. We don't have to find places that take kids, or worry about taking them out of school. It really works for us."

"Really Ginney? I am very unsure. Jerry and I have talked about children, but he doesn't know yet we would have to adopt. I don't think he will mind. I want a family, several kids, a dog, and a picket fence. You know the drill. I want it all."

"In that case, one size does not fit all. We are happy with our freedom, but I do understand that it's not for everyone. I work a shift in emergency and when some mother or father comes in with a kid that is injured, I think, no thanks. Not for me, I'm just not cut out for that. Besides Charlie and I are a family, just a small husband and wife family, but a family none the less."

A marriage without children that was something I had never considered. I came from a family with four kids. Perhaps it was just a mindset. Considering what happened to my family, perhaps Ginney was right. A family is a family, no matter what size, or who is a part of it.

Chapter Nine

I Remember What Happened

Damnedest thing about memory. Just when you think you have remembered everything there is to remember about a person, you remember something else.

This memory is about my Dad. It is not pleasant ... I remember ...

I graduated from the 'Springdale Technical School of Nursing' as a licensed practical nurse. I passed the state board without any trouble. I was now in a position to leave my hometown, where the memories and nightmares had started. I could start a new life, a new beginning, a new town.

I sent my resume to the hospitals in some of the larger cities surrounding our little town. I was hoping that a hospital in the 'Little Rock' area would accept me. If that wish came true, Johnny and I could move there and begin again.

I was still working for Dr Kelly and waiting patiently to hear from any of the hospitals. I had been checking the mail every day at the house. I was hoping and praying for some positive response. To my amazement, there was none. I couldn't understand it. My resume looked pretty good, my grades in school were very good, and I had graduated close to the top of my class. There was no reason for this complete silence, not a word, not a whisper, not even a note to tell me I had been rejected.

Then it happened. I found out it had nothing to do with my resume, or my grades. It was my own father and Bobby Fulton. They had sabotaged my mail. They were determined to control me. They had decided between them, how to stop me from ever getting a job. To tell you the truth, to find out that Bobby would do such a thing didn't surprise me. To find out that my own father, had conspired with him, and against me, was a complete shock!

They had decided this was best for me.

A month after I graduated, dad pleaded with me to come to church with him. They had a new pastor and he wanted me to hear him. I finally gave in, as usual, and went with him.

Johnny and I sat right at the front of the church with dad. Dad's view was that the people, who sat at the back, were hiding from God. He also didn't want anyone to think he was late coming in, as this was another reason for people sitting at the back.

When the preacher started speaking, he said he had a couple of announcements to make. His voice seemed louder than usual.

"Number one, I would like you all to pray for Bobby Fulton, he has been appointed as the new pastor of the 'New Bible Church' in Eastland Heights.

"Number two, Bobby Fulton is to marry Darlene Mason in two weeks. You are all invited to their wedding which will be held here, at our own 'Bible Church.'"

I was absolutely stunned, and could feel my face getting hot. Before I could disagree, dad put his hand over my mouth and dragged me out of the church by my arm. I got loose and stood glaring at him.

"Have you lost your mind?" I asked him.

"Darlene, this is the way it has to be. I have put up with your contrary behavior all this time, because you took good care of my house and my little Johnny. But now, I won't put up with your stubborn ways any more."

He tightened his grip on my arm and pulled me to a bench at the side of the church. He pushed me down hard to the sitting position.

"I'm going to sell my gas station and move to Alaska. I have found a woman, who I want to marry, and that is what I'm going to do."

"But what about momma?" I cried. "You can't marry someone else when you are already married to momma!"

"I divorced your momma years ago Darlene. I just never told you. This is the way it is. If you want to keep Johnny with you, you are going to have to marry Bobby Fulton. Bobby has told me that it's OK with him, if Johnny lives with the two of you. I don't want to take Johnny with me, and well, he would be happier with you."

He took a deep breath, and I knew he wasn't finished with his ultimatum.

"Otherwise, I am sending Johnny to live with Jasper and Selena in Southwest Missouri, and I'll make sure, you never see him again. So make up your mind Darlene, marry Bobby and keep Johnny or lose Johnny forever."

"I don't understand any of this daddy. Is this really what you want?"

"It is."

"I must marry Bobby to keep Johnny with me? How can you treat your own daughter this way?"

I cried and didn't stop for two weeks, but nobody cared. I was in a daze. I went to work and came home. I had no choice in one of the biggest decisions of my life. Dad was telling me how I had to live my life. No, not telling me, forcing me. I didn't like that feeling. Johnny was so sweet, and listened to everything I had to say. If he had not been there, I know I would never have survived.

Mercifully I can't remember the wedding. I'm sure Dad walked me down the aisle, and then handed me over to the enemy. I surely don't remember saying 'I do'. I can't imagine being married, now, or ever to Bobby.

I didn't want to be married at this time in my life. I know I never wanted to be married to Bobby Fulton.

I do remember Bobby and his brothers getting drunk, and ruining the reception. They were rude belching and scratching themselves, and spewing their filthy talk to anyone who would listen. I wanted to run away!

The honeymoon was a disaster. I didn't love this man. I didn't even like him. We spent the night in a little town near where we lived. I didn't know what to expect, but as soon as we arrived at the motel, Bobby hurried me into the room. He slammed the door closed and started ripping my clothes off. He threw me on the bed, dropped his pants, shoved his penis inside me, and started yelling: "I have been waiting a long time to do this to you witch. A long time bitch, do you hear me." There was a hard thrust behind every word.

No words of love or tenderness. He finished his thrusting and rolled off my body. I hurt; I burned inside, and all of my private parts were sore. I bled openly. Bobby pulled the covers up over his head and started snoring. I just lay there, thinking about what had just happened. I felt wounded and dirty.

I quietly went into the bathroom and took a long shower. I wasn't able to wash off the pain and despair. I was bleeding. I sobbed. Is this marriage? Is this it? Is this my life from here on in? I felt trapped and lonely, very lonely.

The next morning, Bobby was up early. We had to clean the church where he was the new pastor, I was told. It was then that I found out the real reason, why Bobby had to marry me so soon. At that time the 'Bible Church' would not allow him to be a Minister, unless he was a married man. There were no single pastors, so our marriage was a fraud from the beginning, in every way.

He was angry when he saw the church; the building was old and run-down. It needed painting, inside and out. There were twelve benches for the potential congregation. The piano was old, with a coat of greasy paint, and out of tune. There were leather-tattered songbooks, and a stage. The pulpit was standing on rotting wood, and looked quite dangerous for anyone to stand on, let alone preach from. There was an old, crumbling, one-legged bench behind the podium. The thick green paint that had been smeared on, still had pieces of the paintbrush showing.

The house where we were supposed to live was even worse. There was no running water. The bathroom was an outside toilet, with a half moon on the rotting door. It wasn't even a toilet; it was a shed that stank to high heavens. Pardon the pun.

When we walked into the horrible house, I saw that dad had dropped off some of my old furniture. He had brought Johnny's bedroom set and mine. He must have delivered it, right after our staged wedding.

There were rat droppings, spiders, and thick webs clung to the walls and the ceilings. I spent the whole week, scrubbing, disinfecting, and scraping dirt off the floor with a putty knife. I was trying my best to make a home for Johnny and I, with a man we both loathed.

The house was just that, a house, never a home.

Bobby said I had to hurry and get the house ready, this would free me up to help him clean the church for Sunday services. We worked from morning till night. Finally the house and church showed some order. In reality, it was two old

Marine barracks, side by side, which I never could get completely clean.

On Sunday there were about twelve people at the church. After services, Bobby met with some of the men. They wanted to choose a board to administer the church. He came into the house after the meeting and announced: "Until the church gets on its feet, I am going to allow you to work for that doctor. We will also act as foster parents for some troubled children. There is a girl coming in a few days. We will be paid by the month, to take care of her. Johnny will have to sleep on the couch."

Bobby never talked anything over with me. He dictated.

I heard his words loud and clear. Bobby would not support Johnny and me. Bobby needed my cheque to live on. Allowing me to work meant that Bobby had no money. I loved to work; I could get away from Bobby and my horrible life. I could work eight hours a day, or more if the doctor would let me.

I took Johnny to school and then I would cross the street to the doctor's office. I also made plans to take some classes at 'Springdale Technical School'. This would be my path to a degree in accounting.

"When do you get paid?" Bobby barked.

"Why?" I asked.

"I will pick it up. I want you to sign your cheque over to me."

"Why?" I asked again.

"Women in the church aren't allowed to own any property or keep any money. You know that bitch."

He slapped me hard. He would never slap me on the face; he would not want to leave marks.

"Don't ask me questions bitch. You ain't got no right. I ain't gonna take crap from you, you hear me? I ain't like your daddy."

I made up my mind that he wasn't going to get my whole cheque. Since I wrote the cheques and managed the office, I decided to deduct something from my pay. I would save that deduction for emergencies, for Johnny and me.

Bobby never worked a day in his life, so he would never know the current wage amount. I decided to call it insurance, for Johnny and me. My plan to keep fifty dollars out of every pay cheque worked. Bobby didn't know.

My wages, and the money from the state, paid for the care of the foster children. We were able to meet our bills and live quite nicely, but I couldn't figure out what Bobby did with the money. He went with me once a month to buy groceries. The state gave us food stamps, so that helped us stretch our budget. They also paid him one hundred and fifty dollars, for each foster child we had.

Our first foster child was a fifteen-year-old girl. She had been picked up on the street as a prostitute, in Little Rock, Arkansas. She had been abused, and had no idea where her family lived. Carol was a sweet girl, and she and I were like mother and daughter.

We had to remodel our home before any foster children were allowed to live with us. We had to have plumbing, even though Bobby was content to do without it. We also had to add a bedroom. The men from the church helped to build the additional bedroom, even donated the materials.

Carol came to our home a year after Bobby and I were married. I loved her company.

Johnny was in school all day and I was now working part-time. Each day I drove them to school in a town nearby, and I went to work. I was taking some accounting classes as well. I was the bookkeeper at Dr Kelly's office, and kept my schoolbooks with Johnny's, so Bobby wouldn't find them. He didn't want me to get any further education, because I made the women at the church feel uncomfortable. I was too smart, and considered a bad example for them.

"Women only need to know, what men want them to know, and that is to stay in their place. They don't need an education to clean a house.

143

Their job is only to take care of their man, and their children." The churchwomen spoke the same lines every day.

That is what Bobby believed and that is what he preached every Sunday.

He gave me the same speech all week.

Bobby wanted to know why I wasn't pregnant. We had sex twice a week, never voluntary on my part, except during my periods. I told him about my disease. The endometriosis was worse when I had my period. I told him he could catch it, if he didn't leave me alone. I also told him he could grow breasts.

He believed me.

I was raising Johnny and three foster children. I would have no energy for my own kids. I didn't want children with Bobby. I didn't want him to be their father.

He would get drunk often, and drive off in his pick-up truck to visit his Aunt Loretta. She was like a mother to him. His aunt was fat and angry most of the time; she also held the family fortune.

Bobby wouldn't come home till morning after visiting his Aunt Loretta.

Bobby's family had an auto-parts mail order business that made them very rich. Maxine was frugal in giving the money to the Fulton family members. She liked to keep most of it for herself.

Thirteen months after we were married, I missed my period. I thought I was pregnant. I told Bobby, he was surprised and showed me some affection. That was not expected and I was taken unawares.

"Check it out with the doc when you go to work on Monday Darlene."

Bobby didn't wait for the results of the pregnancy test. He announced from the pulpit on the Sunday that I was pregnant. I told him I wasn't sure, and that he should have waited. We didn't have the results of the first test and he wanted me to take a second one on the Monday. I told the doctor that Bobby wanted me to take another test. The doctor gave me the second test. He said I was pregnant, but he wasn't sure whether I could carry the baby full term, because of my endometriosis. The doctor wanted to run more tests at the hospital, but I might have to quit work, stay home, and get plenty of rest, to keep the baby. After I told Bobby the news, I told him the risk and what the doctor advised.

"You are just a lazy witch. A lot of women work right through their pregnancies. You have to continue working. That is the only way we can make it around here."

During the second month I miscarried. I was at work when it happened. The doctor told me

145

that the first two or three months were critical. I cried, no wept. I wept and wept and wept.

"Oh doctor, I don't know how to tell Bobby. He has been counting on this baby."

"Well, dear, it wasn't your fault."

He walked out of the room and came back.

"Bring him to the office and I'll explain to him about the miscarriage. While he is here, I will explain to him about your endometriosis."

"No, please don't," I sobbed. "I'll tell him, but I have to pick the right time."

My idea of the right time was when the head of the 'Bible Church' board came to visit. They wanted to see what we had done to the church. There seemed to be an educated man on the board, and he appeared to be an understanding person. When he came into the house and congratulated me on being pregnant, I looked at him and Bobby sadly, and said. "I had a miscarriage at work yesterday. The doctor warned me that this might happen."

The man looked sympathetically at me and smiled warmly.

"There will be many more chances to have a child, my dear. I hear there are a number of women who miscarry during their first pregnancy." He reached over and patted my arm.

I nodded back at him with a weak smile, and glanced at Bobby. He was raging. I knew he would hit me as soon as this dear man was gone. But he acted with complete control, and forced a smile. He knew this man had his future in the palm of his hand. He smiled at him and turned and smiled at me.

"We are going to try again, that is, after she is feeling better."

He looked at me with hate in his eyes when the man wasn't looking.

When the man left, Bobby threw his food on the floor. He said it was the worse food he had ever eaten, and that I had embarrassed him by serving it.

Later that night, Bobby came into our bedroom.

"I bet you killed my child, you witch. I know you didn't want to have a kid with me. You are getting pregnant if I have to fuck you every time I come home. You hear me? You hear me bitch? You have a duty to me, and we are gonna have a baby, one way, or another. We are also gonna have sex, whether you want it or not. You have to obey me. I am your husband and what I say, and do, is right. Do you understand me? Do you get it? Do you hear me witch?"

I knew he was going to hit me. Bobby had huge hands. I tried to protect my face. He made his fist, and knocked me to the floor. He shook his massive fist in my face and grabbed me by the neck. I was dragged across the floor and stuffed into the closet. He shut the door and locked it. I could hear him laughing as he walked away.

Johnny and Carol weren't home. They were over at the neighbour's house.

Bobby left the house; I could hear the front door slam shut.

It was about an hour or so, before I heard Carol and Johnny come into the house. I yelled for them to let me out of the closet. I heard them running all over the house, trying to find out which closet I was in. I heard Johnny's frantic words.

"Darlene, I can't find the key. That a-hole must have it with him."

They beat on the door, kicking it with their feet. Suddenly the door fell off the hinges and Johnny was crying. So was Carol.

"As long as I am living in this house, that man will not do anything to you again. I am not going to let him hurt you. I promise you, I will fight him until one of us is dead." Johnny was sobbing.

We all cried and hugged. Johnny talked so sweetly and bravely. Carol held my hand. She said she only stayed because she loved Johnny and me.

Bobby was mean to Johnny, but not Carol. She was a source of monthly income.

Bobby stumbled into the house later that night, he was drunk. I was half-asleep when he pushed the bedroom door open and slurred: "We are gonna have sex right now. Do you hear me, witch?"

I didn't have the strength to refuse, so I let him get on with it. About one minute later, he got off me. I pushed him, to move him further away from me. He didn't wake up; he fell to the floor naked, and stayed there all night.

When I got up to go to work, I stepped over him. I threw a blanket over his fat, naked body. I didn't want to look at him. I didn't want to see him. He repulsed me.

The state sent us three more foster children, all brothers from the same family. Their father threw some gasoline on a wood burning stove in their trailer home. One of the boys was severely burned, and one of his brothers saved his life. He threw him out of the window into the snow. We took in the two boys for a month and then the badly burned brother, who was in rehab, came to join them. The three brothers were adopted, but needed a home for three months until they went to their new adopted family.

The state gave us a television for the children to watch in the evening, but the church didn't approve of television, radio, or any other kind of entertainment in the home. These machines were inventions of the devil. Since the state provided the television and they paid for it, I saw no harm in letting the children watch it. They loved it. I allowed them to watch it after they had done their homework and chores. I was strict about the viewing times. I definitely didn't think it was a church matter. Apparently, Bobby and the women of the church disagreed.

One Thursday night, four churchwomen marched into my home, led by Bobby. They pulled the plug out of the television, causing protests from the children and me; they carried it outside and smashed it. Johnny and I tried to stop them, but Bobby threw a dictionary at him. He grabbed hold of Johnny and sat on him. The result was that Johnny ended up with a broken rib.

The churchwomen grabbed me by the hair and threw me against the wall. The foster children were hysterical, crying and pleading for Bobby and the women to stop hurting me. Bobby laughed when the women took turns at swinging me around and letting me go. They would hurl me into the furniture and walls. My arms and sides were aching. One of them, I think her name was Mattie, banged my head on the wall and yelled: "You had the devil's box in your home, and you are poisoning the children's minds. You have to be punished; your husband Preacher Bobby said so."

Two women held me while another woman punched me in the stomach. They twisted my arms behind my back and slapped me, again and again. Bobby stood smiling approvingly, egging them on. I was barely conscious and in terrible pain, I begged them to stop.

"I told you before witch. You aren't living with your dad any more. You are my property now and you are going to obey my rules. I am not going to have that devil's box in my house, you hear me?" Bobby screamed.

He made a fist to hit me, but before he could hit me again, Johnny jumped on his back and began to pound him with his fists. Bobby shook him off easily, but Johnny got back on his feet and stood his ground.

"I told you, Bobby, I don't want you to ever touch my sister again. I don't care if you are bigger than I am. We are going to fight this out, right here, right now." Johnny was white with anger.

Bobby laughed. He reached out and pulled Johnny off his feet. He punched him in the face and threw him around the room. When Johnny fell, Bobby kicked him in his back, dragging him around with his legs spread, stepping on his arms. Johnny curled up in a ball and tried to protect himself.

Johnny had smashed teeth, a second broken rib and a broken arm. I gathered him up with the children's help, and we took him to the car. I drove him to the emergency room. I had no idea what to say to the doctor's. I couldn't lie. He wasn't in an automobile accident, he didn't fall.

The doctor's smelled abuse, I knew it. They took Johnny to a separate room. The police sat down and questioned him. A half hour later, they talked to me.

"Ma'am, your brother has pressed charges against your husband. We are going to arrest him."

I was torn between Johnny and the fear of what Bobby would do, if we had him arrested. I didn't care what happened to Bobby. I hated him. But I was sure as soon as he got out of jail, he would probably kill both of us.

I had to protect Johnny. He would have to leave. I felt I could take care of myself. I told the police where I lived, and they left. I went in to see Johnny.

"Johnny, honey, I'm scared. I have to find you somewhere safe. Bobby is going to jail. He will probably only be there for a few days. Aunt Maxine will pay his bond. I know she will."

"Darlene, you gotta get out of there." Johnny was crying and pleading with me.

"Please leave Darlene, please, I beg you. That guy is crazy."

"Johnny, I made a commitment. I promised the Lord that I would be married to Bobby, 'till death do us part'. I have to live up to my promise. It is an agreement between God and me. I'm obligated Johnny, can't you see that. It will get better, it will, he will settle down. He will change Johnny; he will change after this, after being in jail. I'm sure he will."

I lied to Johnny to keep him calm. If he killed Bobby, he would go to prison and I would never forgive myself. On the other hand, if Bobby killed Johnny, I would also not be able to live with myself.

I was so mixed up in a sick manipulation of fear, and survival. I didn't say any more.

Bobby would only be in jail for a few days. I needed to find a place for Johnny to live. I ran into my doctor friend at the hospital, he was on his rounds. I knew I could trust him.

"Dr Kelly, I need to ask you a big favour."

"Hi Darlene. How is Johnny?"

I started to cry. I told him what had happened with Bobby and the fight. He listened quietly.

"I have an extra room in my home Darlene. Johnny may stay there as long as he needs to for his own safety."

Dr Kelly had such a calming effect on me. The doctor was a selfless man. He had helped me so many times and in so many ways.

I didn't know what I was going to do about Bobby. I was so thankful that I had people in my life, like Dr Kelly. I cried, thanked him, and gave him a huge hug. He smiled. He never gave me advice. He only ever listened and helped. I respected him so much.

As we drove home from the hospital, we passed the police car coming back from the house. Bobby was in the back seat. He saw Johnny and me. He looked menacingly at us. I was terrified.

So, now I knew. Dad wasn't telling me everything. There was more, and I had remembered some of it. He had made me marry Bobby Fulton; he threatened me with losing Johnny to some of my other relatives. How could he do that? I struggled to understand why he would treat me that way?

There is no explanation good enough ... for what he did to me.

Chapter Ten

Jerry

Jerry was one of those guys. I remembered meeting him and liking him right away. He was one of those fellows, who knew just what to say to a woman, and when to say it.

I remember talking to him about my former husband, and him listening so intently, to every word. He was kind and gentle and very attentive. Something that I had never had, someone who seemed to focus on 'just me', rather than his own likes and dislikes. He wasn't a young man, but then he wasn't an old man either. He seemed very safe.

He started coming up to the hospital regularly to see me. He never just dropped in, but would always call before he came. It was fun. He would come to the room and we would talk. He was helping me to remember my former life, and whatever he was doing, was helping me tremendously. I was remembering things that I had totally forgotten.

When he first started visiting, he would help me into my wheelchair, and take me all over the hospital. We would just talk, and talk, for hours during the visit.

Then later, when I began using my canes, he would help me along my way. He would walk with me very slowly. We would stop here and there. He made me laugh.

I was several months in rehab, when he asked me if I remembered anything, right before the 'incident'. I looked at him with a very blank expression.

"Well, do you Darlene?" He asked.

"Not really Jerry."

"You and I are married Darlene."

I must say I didn't expect that. I didn't take the news very well. I almost folded right there and then, on the main floor of the hospital.

"Married? Why didn't anyone tell me?"

"Because, you are still in rehabilitation. I didn't want to spring anything on you. I was worried it might cause a reaction, much like I'm seeing here right now." He helped me over to the chair as he spoke.

"I am ... speechless Jerry. And this time it isn't because of my memory. I thought we were just talking about getting married. Isn't that what we have been talking about for the last few weeks?" I asked him.

"Yes of course, but, well, Dr Norman and your dad, they both thought that too much information at the one time might create a problem. So we decided to handle it the way we did. Rightly or wrongly so, Darlene, we did what we thought was best."

"Well, then. I guess my future is not for me to figure out then. I ... we ... what are we going to do?" I asked.

"Before the .... the ... thing, I mean the 'incident', we were, em ... going to move to Florida. I'm tired of this climate, and we had decided that we would go down there, and enjoy the weather. We also decided it would be a great place to enjoy each other. And, well, enjoy married life, as a couple."

"Wow! Wow! Jerry, I don't remember this at all." I got up from the chair and looked at him for a moment.

"Take me back to my room please; I need some time to think."

"Right." He was not amused.

We went to my room.

Things were suddenly moving too fast for me, I felt like I was caught up in a whirl-wind, rather than real life. I was somewhat

157

numb, from finding out that I was married. I couldn't understand why no-one had told me.

I didn't remember Jerry, at least not that much of him. And, I guess, this was all too much for my brain to process.

The cloak of depression climbed over my shoulders for about three days. Dr Norman stopped all of my sessions with the therapists. She ordered me to rest and relax in my room. Ginney was to take me on long walks around the gardens outside.

"For heaven's sake Darlene, use the wheelchair for a while. I know that you have been pushing to stand up and be normal, but you are going to have to slow down some. I want you to be able to get out of here as soon as possible, but you can't push yourself so hard. You might have a relapse." Ginney was shaking her head.

"Relapse? To what?" I asked slowly.

"To, well, there is a chance you might seize Darlene, or perhaps your brain might totally reject all the progress you have made. With injuries as serious as you have, well, the truth is, we really don't know what might happen. I just want you to be very careful, and stop pushing yourself so hard. Just relax, and let things happen as they are supposed to." Ginney smiled a little, and we made our way back to my room. The doctor was waiting for us.

Doctor, I'm a married woman, did you know that? I just found out, and no-one bothered to tell me. Jerry is my husband! I have to get out of here. I need to take care him, and of course, my house. I'm supposed to do as a wife does. I'm feeling very restrained in here, I should be doing better." I was almost shouting at her.

"Look, Darlene. There is no short-cut to your getting well. And I do understand it is frustrating, but, if you don't slow down, there are going to be serious consequences. I don't intend to let that happen, so you might as well relax. All right? I mean it Darlene, you will have to slow down." Dr Norman left the room.

She was right of course. I was becoming too impatient. The flooding in of all those memories and the memories that hadn't come back yet, were making me very uptight. She was right. I knew she was right. I did have to relax. I reasoned with myself for a while and then Ginney interrupted my thoughts.

"What's up Darlene, as if I didn't know?"

"Well, we are just going to have to relax Ginney." I said with some sarcasm as I mimicked the good doctor.

"Well Darlene, that means we are going to the gardens, so get in the wheelchair, and no arguments about it. You are riding, not walking. I have my orders too you know." Ginney aided me to the wheelchair.

So for the next few days, Ginney and I were viewing the gardens and I was riding around in the wheelchair. Not my favourite thing, but orders are orders. And heaven knows I didn't want to delay my chances of getting out.

My biggest hurdle at that point was getting over the fact that I was a married lady. I was trying to put everything in perspective.

I did find out that my former room-mate Anne, was still in town, but she had never came to the hospital to see me. I called her.

"Anne, this is Darlene. Where have you been?" I said in my most cheerful voice.

"Darlene! Is that you, Darlene? I can't believe it, is it really you. I'm so sorry. I should have been up to see you, but when I read the papers and heard on the news all that had happened to you, I felt like it was my fault. I should never have left you alone on that bike trail."

"Your fault Anne? Why on earth would it be your fault? My ex- husband hired those men and ..." Anne jumped in and stopped me finishing.

"I know, but you were alone. There was no reason for that, except I was being me. Don't you blame me Darlene?" Anne was almost crying now.

"No, well, maybe a little. But, I'll get over it. Really I will. Now, you come up and see me. I'm trying to get my memory and my life back, and I need my friends to help me."

"Wow! OK Darlene. I will be there tomorrow afternoon, how will that be?"

"That will just be great Anne."

We talked a bit more and then we hung up. She seemed like a nice person. I really didn't remember much about her, at the time. But, maybe she would help me to add some more information, to my memories.

The next day Anne came to the hospital. I thought I would know her when I saw her. But the old memory buttons weren't working too well that particular day. I didn't recognise her at all. I didn't have a clue.

She came over to the wheelchair and gave me a hurried hug, and then sat down in one of the chairs in the room. She smiled in a nervous sort of a way, and asked. "How ... um are you?"

"Oh, much better than I look. Today is one of those 'not so good' days. I have them now and then." I answered.

"I thought Jerry said you were walking." She was staring at the wheelchair.

"I was. The doctor thought perhaps I was moving too fast, and condemned me back to that thing for a while. She thought it wouldn't be as much stress on me. She worries about me being stressed. Something to do with the, um ... accident."

"It wasn't an accident Darlene. It was two guys who tried to kill you." Anne was shaking her head as she continued.

"I should have never gone off and left you alone. I had no idea that anyone was even thinking about hurting you. Honest Darlene, honest, if I had only known." The look of guilt on Anne's face was making me feel sad.

"Wait a minute Anne. Those guys did try to kill me, and I'm not even sure why. You had nothing to do with it. You are feeling guilty for no reason, no reason at all. While I realise you did go on without me, I ... that part of it ... well. Look, it's over. The guys are all in jail; my ex-husband is in jail. And

I'm getting better. So forget it, for your own sake."

"Thank you so much Darlene, for saying all that. Really, how are you doing?" Anne's voice was calmer now.

"Very well, all things considered. I have a problem with my memory; they say that my short term memory might never be what it used to be. I have other problems, with my balance, thought process, things like that. But, in all, I'm really doing well."

"Good for you Darlene. How's Jerry?"

"You know Anne, that's sort of an interesting question. I really didn't remember having married him. He told me just last week. I was really surprised, to say the least, and somewhat taken aback. I ... um, eh, he seems like a nice fellow. But I don't know.

He said you were at the wedding, and dad and Nelda were there too. Apparently all the folks that I worked with were there. I really don't remember. The only wedding I remember was to Bobby Fulton. I'm not ... em ...

They have me in here as Darlene Fulton. I guess I haven't changed the name on my accounts, or driver's license. Maybe dad gave them that name. I really don't know. I just thought it was strange, really strange Anne. I haven't gotten used to the idea yet."

"Has Gerry been up here a lot?"

"He has been coming up for the last month or so, but I was here for a while before he showed up. He never said one word to me, about being married I mean. That's why I was so shocked."

"That's sort of odd Darlene, don't you think? Are you still going to Florida with him, when you get out of here?"

"I don't know. We haven't talked about that."

"Well I had better go Darlene, you better rest or whatever. Call me if you need anything."

Anne was gone.

The meeting with Anne was strained. I suppose part of the reason was her feeling of guilt. She felt she was partially responsible for what had happened to me.

I didn't blame her for the 'incident'. I'm sure those guys would have thrown *her* off the cliff along with me, had she been there. So perhaps it was a blessing that she wasn't. All things work out for the best. Right?

Chapter Eleven

Out Of One Prison In To Another

Jerry's hospital visits became more regular. He was getting more anxious about the time I would have to stay in hospital. He wanted us to get on with our lives together. I wasn't sure that I wanted to go to Jerry's home, or what was supposed to be our home, but I sure did want out of that hospital.

It was another month before Dr Norman agreed to consider letting me leave.

I was now going to a counsellor once every few days, plus all the rehab. I was stretching and bending, and doing everything that I was supposed to do physically. The nurse who was helping me with my reading and writing, was really pleased with my returning abilities, and gave me the green light to go.

Of course I had to agree to return every few days and visit the counsellor, and the other folks that were stipulated. But at least I could be on my own, part of the time.

So, the day finally came, and Jerry was excited that I was coming home.

Dad and Nelda were there to cheer me on as well. Dr Norman loaded me down with papers full of instructions. She had drawn up a schedule for all the various therapy sessions and appointments I would need to keep.

That last day, my favourite nurse Ginney wheeled me out the door. It was a strange feeling, a combination of relief and joy. I was so happy to be going anywhere, other than back to that dreary hospital room. I couldn't wait to get out. I couldn't believe I was actually leaving.

Dad and Nelda walked beside me, and Jerry was almost skipping.

Dr Norman joined the parade. There were nurses' lined up along the hall, and they were all saying goodbye, and waving. Some of them had a tear in their eye.

Some of the other patients, and visitors, had no idea what was going on. They were looking around for a dignitary, or celebrity of some kind.

Ginney explained to everyone in a very loud voice, that she, for one, never thought I would be leaving the hospital. She went on to explain that it was a miracle I had recovered at all, and how astonishing it was that I was in such good shape.

Then Dr Norman said a few words. She told everyone how proud she was, to be a part of my recovery. She also recommended that I stayed away from high places for a while! Everyone laughed, me included.

Anne came, just in time to join the crowd of well-wishers. And so my life was complete, my recovery was real, and I was going home!

Jerry's car was waiting for me at the front door. As I got in, dad, Nelda and Anne said they would see me at home.

When I arrived at Jerry's house, I really didn't know where I was. But I put on a happy, brave face. I felt really strange when I walked through the door. It was obvious Jerry had cleaned the place from top to bottom. There wasn't a speck of dust to be seen anywhere. He had gone to the bakery and picked up a 'welcome home' cake, it looked so sweet. He set out some ice and drinks, and everyone made themselves at home.

I had a piece of cake with some pop, and suddenly felt extremely tired. I made my excuses and went to lie down for a while. The excitement had been too much for me.

I slept.

When I woke up I heard voices. I realised dad and Nelda were still in the front room.

I was making my way along the hall when I heard dad speaking.

"When I first saw her Jerry, I didn't think she was going to be with us at all."

"Well, thanks dad. That makes my day!" I said with a smile and a little laugh.

"You were in bad shape baby. It's a real miracle that you are here at all. Just think about it." Dad's voice was soft.

"Yeah, I guess so." I replied.

I sat down and had another piece of cake. This was a rare event for me, getting near a cake; in the hospital my menu was guarded, and sweets and cakes were not allowed.

I was happy. I was surrounded by my friends and family, and safe in my own home. But would it last?

I was having regular memory sessions, with and without a doctor. I had now remembered almost everything about my life before the cliff incident.

The most traumatic memories were those of the abuse and horror of living with Bobby Fulton. I remembered almost every day with him. His endless preaching, about how women were nothing but servants for their men. I kept thinking about him saying that no-one would ever want me, except him. I remembered him ranting about not having children, and yelling and screaming at me.

I suppose you must be asking yourself, and not for the first time in reading this book, 'why didn't she leave him'? Well, how many times do you think I have asked myself, that same question? 'Why on earth didn't I leave him?'

My counsellors and I concluded, it was FEAR. I was afraid to. What a very simple answer? He had bent my mind so out of shape, that I believed everything he told me. I believed that I was not capable of taking care of myself, without him. I believed he was the only man who would ever put up with me. Eventually, I fully believed exactly what the church, and its pastor *Bobby Fulton* preached every Sunday. I believed that as a woman, I had no rights. I also eventually believed that I was not allowed to own anything in my own name, and God put me here on this earth, to serve my man.

And so I did, for many years.

My memory was now coming back to me in large doses. I would hear something, or smell a certain smell, and a whole part of my memory would come flooding back.

Jerry was getting worried as these memory patches would overwhelm me. I would blank out in the middle of a conversation, or in the middle of doing a chore around the house. When I came out of the blank, that part of time in the present, had gone missing.

Such a time happened in the middle of one of my home days. Jerry was at work. I remember smelling the wonderful scent of baking bread. The smell, reminded me, of one of the most horrible times of my life.

I sat down, and my memory bank began to play.

I had been living in some sort of a la-la land with Bobby. I had just accepted the fact that this was how my life was going to be from now on. I had accepted that Bobby was going to rule my life, and my life was going to be spent making him happy.

I had long given up on the idea, of having children. The thought of bringing an unsuspecting child into our house through adoption, was not something I would even consider. After all, I was aware Bobby was a sexual predator, and an abuser. How could I think about bringing a child into that?

One day, I finally came to my senses and realised what was happening around me. I had driven home from work, and found the yard full of trucks, most of which I recognised as belonging to Bobby's relatives.

I remember peering in the window of the front room, and trying to see what was going on. I saw all of Bobby's brothers and sisters-in-law, standing around drinking beer, and talking. And oh, yes, there was Aunt Loretta.

Aunt Loretta was the woman who had taken Bobby and his brothers in, when their father had murdered their mother. She was a sister of his father's, but somehow the wisdom of the judicial system, had allowed her to keep the boys. Had they understood that she was an extension of her brother, perhaps they would have reconsidered their decision. She was a mean, heartless woman. She had never married, probably because she couldn't get along with anyone for very long! She had raised the boys, more or less. Actually, she had allowed them to do what they wanted, when they wanted. She belonged to the church! In fact, she was a major reason for my father believing that my marrying Bobby, was a good idea.

She visited my dad regularly, and told him what a good guy Bobby was. She had a real hand in getting dad to join the church. She supported without question, everything the boys' did. This included beating their wives, or stealing from *their neighbours. Those boys' could do no wrong, in her eyes.*

So, I had to ask myself, why was she here? Why was she in my house, at night? I could only think of one way to find out. So I braced myself, and walked in the front door.

I was not ready for what was about to happen. I don't think anyone would be in my place.

As soon as I got through the door, one of Bobby's brothers grabbed me. He twisted my hands behind my back, and sat me down hard on a wooden chair.

He twisted a rope around me, securing me to the chair. It was almost impossible for me to breathe, much less move. I gasped for air, and the whole bunch of them marched around me. They took turns at telling me of something I had done, to transgress against Bobby. It was really weird. It was as if I was in some kind of a strange, witch type ritual. It was like something you would see in a movie, not in real life.

I was confused; I didn't understand what was going on.

Loretta's turn to pass me was saved until last.

"You went against God and Bobby. You had an operation, to stop you having his child!" This was a growl coming out of Aunt Loretta, not a voice.

"No, no, no, I didn't. I had to have that operation, it saved my life." I protested.

Bobby pushed Aunt Loretta aside, and started yelling at me.

"You are a liar and a cheat. You are a bitch; you are a horrible, dishonorable bitch! You have lied to me. You have told nothing but lies our entire married life. You are now going to pay for those lies. That's right bitch, you are now going to pay God and me. You owe us." His face was contorted with bitterness and rage.

Then, he hit me so hard on the face, that I felt dizzy, and sick.

This was obviously the cue, for the rest of them to join in. They all started hitting and beating me. I don't even remember what they used; I passed out shortly after Bobby hit me across the face.

When I awoke, I was in a bed, in a room that I had never seen. I didn't know how I got there and couldn't figure out why I was there.

I would learn that Bobby and his relatives owned this place.

Bobby came in and stood over me, he was laughing. He walked up and removed the rope from my hands. He moved my hands over my head, and tied the rope again, only tighter this time, if that was possible. He started unzipping his pants.

"Now, I'm gonna give you something that you really deserve bitch."

He climbed on top of me. I tried to roll away from him, but he had bound my hands so tightly, it was impossible. He ripped open my legs, and shoved himself inside me, he began what I knew wouldn't take him very long.

In a few minutes he rolled off me, and then hollered: "OK guys, come and get it! She's all warmed up for you. You all need to see what a sorry ride she is."

One by one, the brothers took their turn on top of me.

I wanted to die. I wanted to be sick. I could feel the vomit rise in my throat. I wanted to turn my face away but I couldn't. I was tied to the bed. I kept trying to close my legs, but they would just wrench them open again. I tried to scream, but the gag in my mouth made it sound more like a groan.

In a crazy sort of a way, it seemed like the more I tossed my body from side to side, the more they seemed to enjoy it.

They were rough, clumsy, and drunk. They licked my face and hair like animals. Their stinking tongues and their stinking breath, made my stomach rise to my throat. Their sweating bodies heaved in and out of me.

I wanted to pass out; I knew if I passed out I wouldn't feel any more pain or humiliation. I prayed to God to let me die. If I died before the next brother mounted me, I would feel no more.

They were eventually finished. They had savagely emptied their whole family seed, from every brother, into my body.

I was numb, I knew I was hurt physically, but my mind was hurting more.

Bobby came back in the room, threw some towels on the bed, and untied me. He pulled me up.

"Here you go bitch, clean yourself up whore. That is the last of the good stuff you get from me."

I crawled, yes crawled, into the dirty bathroom, and thought back to my 'wedding night'. I remembered how I had wanted to wash Bobby off of me. I could never have imagined, having to wash all of his brothers off of me as well.

I wanted to wash all of them off of me now. I wanted to wash myself away, away to another place in time. Away to another life, anyone's life, anywhere. It had to be better than mine. I took the cheap soap and scrubbed and scrubbed, I just kept scrubbing. I could see the blood running down my legs but I didn't care, I just scrubbed some more. I only stopped scrubbing when my arms were exhausted. They just wouldn't scrub any more.

I went back to the bed and looked around the room. I ripped the sheets off, as if that would put the whole thing behind me. It would remove the sperm, vomit, and blood from offending my eyes. I looked for clean sheets, and found some yellow ones in a cupboard. I changed the bed.

The door jerked open, it was Bobby.

"Now listen up bitch, you are staying here for the rest of your life. Aunt Loretta will tell you what to do. Starting in the morning, you will work, eat, and sleep right here. You will never see that lousy brother, or any of your family, ever again! You hear me? You hear me bitch?" He stepped closer to me. "You answer me bitch, you answer me whore when I talk to you?"

"I hear you." I mumbled under my breath.

He slammed the door behind him as he left.

I didn't know what to think. I just knew, I would have to get to Johnny. I knew I would have to get to someone. I needed to think, but I couldn't. The movie of the brothers climbing on and off me, kept playing over and over in my mind.

The next few months I wasn't able to do anything. I was like the walking dead, a zombie, a living dead person.

I worked when they told me. I drove the tractor when they told me. I guess they must have shown me how to drive it, as I knew I hadn't driven one before. I didn't care, I just did what I was told, when I was told to do it.

Aunt Loretta sat on the front porch and supervised my ploughing the field. I helped with the hay, and cleaned out the chicken house. Feeding the cows and pigs was also part of my daily chores.

They gave me some old torn blue jeans to wear, that must have belonged to the boys at one time. I had to put a rope around them to hold them up. The knees were worn through and the pockets were hanging off.

Months went by. Winter turned to spring and planting began again.

They didn't allow me to go off the property and slowly I gave up trying, to keep track of time. All I knew now were the seasons. Summer was here again, and that meant I had been in this place for more than a year.

One day, one of the sisters-in-laws', came to the field with Aunt Loretta.

"You come on in now Darlene. You need some work clothes and maybe a dress. You need to look better now." The sister-in-law said.

I looked at myself in the cracked mirror that stood in my bedroom. She was right; I had lost a tremendous amount of weight due to the heavy work. The blue jeans I wore to work were long past there best. So I put myself together, as best I could, and prepared myself for town.

I reluctantly got in the truck with them.

Well, you didn't think for one minute they would let me go on my own, did you?

We went to town, and I ended up in a dress shop on my own. I couldn't believe it. I didn't want to just run up to the sales staff, as I wasn't sure if they were watching me. So I took two dresses to the dressing room, and then created a bit of a fuss. The salesgirl came to see what was going on.

"Go and call my brother Johnny. He's a deputy in the sheriff's department. Tell him that Darlene is here, and she needs to see him. It's urgent. Please, please listen to me. I don't have much time."

The salesgirl looked at me a little strangely at first. But I think she realised quickly by my tone and fear, that I was seriously in need of some help. She took off, and I stood in the dressing room shaking like a leaf. I wasn't sure if she was going for Johnny, or going for Aunt Loretta and her squad.

She obviously believed me, as the next thing I heard, was Johnny yelling for me. I recognised his voice, and ran out of the dressing room with one of the dresses on. The girl looked at me and said: "Miss, you can't leave without paying for that dress." If it wasn't such a terrifying situation, I would have laughed. Johnny quickly threw some dollar bills on the counter, and asked if that would cover it.

She replied. "Yes."

We ran out of the dress shop and straight to Johnny's police car.

"My God Darlene, what is going on? Are you OK? How are you? Where have you been?"

I told him the whole miserable story, well, most of it.

His eyes were popping out of his head: "I should arrest the whole bunch of them Darlene. Right now!"

"No Johnny, no. They'll kill me. No, they'll kill you. Oh! Johnny, they might kill both of us. I mean it, they are crazy, all of them."

We talked a little more, and I told him I was too scared for both of us. I convinced him not to arrest them and let me go back. I told him it was for the best, and assured him I was in no immediate danger. He believed me.

I went back with Aunt Loretta and the girls to my own personal prison. I couldn't take the risk of them getting back at Johnny, if he had arrested them. I couldn't have lived with that. It was easier for me to live in the Fulton prison, than to take the chance.

I stayed there for another six or seven months and did as I had been doing, since I got there.

I took my beatings regularly, and handled the abuse on a daily basis. It had become a way of life for me.

In the eight month, they took the beatings too far. I had the one beating 'that broke the camel's back', so to speak.

That night as I crawled on all fours to get to my bed, I decided I had had enough. I would take no more.

I watched and waited, and watched and waited, for the perfect time to escape. I didn't have to wait too long. They drank themselves in to a stupor this particular night, and fell asleep. I made sure they were all out of it, and decided, it was time to go. It was now or never.

I got my stuff together, and quickly called the sheriff's office. I lowered my voice to a whi-. sper. "Can I speak to Johnny?" The voice on the other end of the phone, told me Johnny wasn't there. I cried and started to panic. "Please help me, please, please! My name is Darlene Fulton; I am out at the Fulton place. Johnny Mason is my brother. I need help. Please ask Johnny to come and get me. Please ... please ... please ...

We will be there right away ma'am." The voice on the other end of the line, hung up.

I crept out of the house and hid in the barn. I was shaking, my whole body was trembling. I crouched behind a bale of hay, and waited for the sheriff.

They came quicker that I expected. I could see a female officer walking through the yard. She was shining a flashlight. I opened the barn door and waved, and she hurried over to where I was.

I was told later, I didn't look too well.

The female officer grabbed me, and we ran to a car. She pushed me inside.

There was blood in my hair, and all over my clothes.

My brother Johnny ran over to the car window, and told the driver to take me to the women's shelter.

The driver put the car in gear and drove away at speed. I looked back through the window of the car, to see Bobby and his family being herded out of the house. They had their hands on top of their heads and guns pointed at them. I took a deep breath.

"Darlene, Darlene honey! Darlene!"

I heard Jerry yelling at me from a distance. I blinked my eyes and he was standing right in front of me.

"Oh, Jerry." I got up and put my arms around him, and held him close.

"What was it this time Darlene?" He asked quietly.

"I remembered being held captive by those horrible people."

"Hold on, hold on, I'm here now. Don't cry." He held me close.

I gulped in some air, and sat back down on the chair.

"I'm not too sure that these memories are really good for me." I was struggling to get my breath.

"I know Darlene, but Doctor Norman said they would happen more frequently, until you gained back a major portion of your memory. I know how terrible this must be for you. You need to rest now honey. I'll go fix dinner and you just relax." He headed towards the kitchen.

Later that same night, he quietly asked me: "What would you think about us moving to Florida?"

"Oh, I would love it. I like it here, but I've always wanted to live in Florida. I do hate to leave dad though. He and I are just getting to know each other again. You know there was about ten years or so that we weren't on the best of terms?"

"I know that Darlene, but I have the chance of a new job. It will be good money for us. Well, I'm not getting any younger, and I think it's a good deal, for the both of us."

"Where in Florida were you thinking? I need to see if I can get some referrals to the doctors there. I would want to keep up my therapy."

"Cypress Gardens. It's a beautiful, warm, sunny place Darlene. And when you are better, we'll get to finding that child that you've always wanted, or maybe even two. Who knows?" Gerry's voice was happy.

"Cypress Gardens, that sounds just wonderful, and children." I jumped up, put my arms around his neck, and kissed him. "Oh Jerry, that would make me so happy!"

And so, we agreed. Jerry would go down first, and make all the arrangements for us.

He found a beautiful home, and signed the contract for his new job. He called me on the telephone from the new house. "Honey, it's time to come on down. We have a beautiful new house; I think you'll love it, I'm ready to start my new job."

"OK, I'll say my goodbyes to everyone and be down on Monday. I'll call you with the plane schedule. And Jerry, I love you, I love you, I love you."

"And I love you too Darlene." He hung up.

The doctor gave me all the referrals that I needed. I said a tearful goodbye to dad and Nelda. My friend Anne took me to the airport on the Monday morning.

That was my time in Alaska.

It was over.

Chapter Twelve

Florida!

And baby makes ... two!

The moment I saw our new house in Florida, I felt 'at home'. It was cosy. I loved the warmth of the day, and the openness of the house. It was great.

The flowers bloom there all year round. The green of the trees and the grass was a welcome sight, after being stuck in Alaska for so long.

I was feeling more like myself these days. I hadn't felt so well for months. I was laughing a lot and dressing like a modern woman.

Jerry was enjoying the new me. I was transformed almost immediately.

We had new friends, and Jerry loved his new job. We went out a lot, and I was really enjoying being a young woman again.

Jerry and I talked at great length about adoption. He seemed to be very much for it, and his only worry was, how I would react to having to care for a child. I consulted my new counsellor about it. Jerry insisted he talk to her as well, just to make sure that everyone was giving me the 'green light'.

The memory thing was not coming blurred any more. It was now coming in living colour. I was a little worried, but I knew as quickly as these 'memory flashes' would come on, they could go away just as quickly. I suppose it was because I had remembered almost everything by now.

There were many things about my earlier life that bothered me, and I talked them out with my counsellor.

I wondered why I stayed in that damaging relationship with Bobby Fulton. The counsellor told me, she thought there were many reasons; I had been brainwashed by Bobby and all his relatives to accept whatever they said as law. My own good sense might have surfaced now and then, but with their constant grinding on and on, I couldn't hear my own thoughts.

There was also my coming from a male dominated household, where dad's rule was law. I had no normal interaction with a female or mother. I had no woman in my life from the age of eleven. This apparently, had a great deal to do with my attitude toward Bobby. It contributed to my thinking that he was all powerful.

And then the intervention of that church. The beliefs they held, and drummed into my brain, day after day. The churchwomen reinforcing everything that Bobby and his family were saying, added credibility in my mind, to their beliefs.

Then witnessing my own mother leave our household. This to me was wrong, and I believed if I left my own household, then I would be as guilty as she was. I also believed if I left, I would be as hurtful as she had been to me.

So this was some of the answers I was given, as to why I stayed in the relationship with Bobby.

Surely, there was more to it.

The only thing that was bothering me now, was the intense headaches. I was experiencing them every few days. They totally incapacitated me for the entire day. I would drink tons of herbal tea, or go to the beach and sit quietly. If that didn't work, I would sit in a dark room, and listen to soothing music. Jerry worried about my days of headaches, and taking care of a child. But I convinced him, that my need for a child for so long, far outweighed his concern for my bad days. I knew I could take care of a child, and I told him so. I think he felt my intense longing. He was under-standing of my feelings that with children there was a family.

We began visiting various agencies in the area. After many weeks and many questions by directors and caseworkers, we were fin-ally certified as 'acceptable' future parents.

Now all we had to do was wait, and wait we did.

After what seemed like months, but was in actual fact just a few weeks, one of the agencies called.

"Mrs. March? This is Mrs. Douglas, with the Sea Side adoption agency."

"Oh!" I said, trying to compose myself.

"Mrs. March. We have received a child. There are several things I need to tell you before we go any further." Mrs. Douglas sounded very official.

"What are they?" I asked.

"Well, he is a mixed race child, and his mother was a 'crack' user, while she carried him. There might be some issues with him when he gets older."

"I ... em ... em ... what does that mean?" I asked.

"His mother used crack cocaine during her pregnancy, and the child has some prob-lems. We have gotten him passed his own addiction, and he is doing well in that regard. But he continues to have some behavioural problems, and he is a somewhat nervous child."

"Is there anything else I should know?" I asked, wondering what I would tell Jerry.

"His mother is gone, she died of an overdose when little Roger was only six months old. He has been in the system for a little while. We did have him with a foster parent, but they had their hands full with five other kids. It wasn't a good situation for Roger, or the foster family."

"I think we can handle it Mrs. Douglas." As I was saying it, my confidence was draining.

"Let me call my husband, I will get back to you as soon as possible." I hung up the phone.

I dialed Jerry.

He was less than responsive when I told him about little Roger.

"He will need more time than you can give him Darlene. Your own health is not fully restored yet. I think we should pass on this one." Gerry was quite short with me.

"Can't we just go and see him?" I almost begged.

"I don't think that's a good idea Darlene. I've been thinking about it, and I'm just not that sure I'm really cut out to be a father. I mean, I'm not as young as you Darlene, and I'm more set in my ways. It's a big responsibility being a father; my dad wasn't that great a role model. I don't know, I just don't know."

"Let's just go and meet him. Who knows, maybe you will fall in love with him and want to bring him home. At least give it a try, will you, Jerry? Please, will you?"

Finally, he relented. It was more to make me happy than anything else.

Dear Jerry, when I think of him now, he was one of the most generous men I had ever met. But when Roger moved in with us, he was also one of the most selfish men I had ever known.

When we married Jerry knew that we were both older. He also knew that I had been married before. I think with hindsight, he believed, or hoped, it was just going to be the two of us. He had never mentioned children, but I wanted him to know that I couldn't have any. Well at least not in the conventional way. He dismissed the whole subject and that was more or less that.

But later that evening, I told him how much I longed for a child. My dream marriage had always been two people getting together and having a baby, or perhaps two, or three. After all, I was one of four children myself. Children always meant happiness to me. They made a house a 'real home'. He understood, or at least I thought he did.

We met Roger. He was a small child for his age, with dark brown eyes and long eyelashes. He had a timid little smile that was so endearing. I wanted to sign the papers there and then, and take him home to be our baby, but the agency had other plans.

Because Roger was 'special needs', we were only allowed to visit him at the home for an hour or two. This was once a week, increasing to twice a week. We were then allowed to visit him for a full day. This progressed to us taking him home with us, for a weekend visit.

We got to know his little ways, and how sweet his disposition was. He began to get somewhat attached to us. He would cry his little eyes out when we took him back to the home. I was annoyed that we couldn't keep him home for good. But then I convinced myself, that the agency folks knew best.

Jerry was disappointed that little Roger wasn't exactly like other children. When Roger was with us, I didn't have much time for anyone else. At least not as much time as Jerry was looking for. He also voiced his opinion about Roger having special needs, and that he wouldn't grow up and be like other children of his age. Jerry was looking for all the reasons he could find, to prevent us from adopting Roger.

I was certain I could get Jerry to change his mind. I was convinced when little Roger came to live with us and we were a real family, Jerry would have a different point of view.

I wanted Roger to be ours so badly. I convinced myself that Jerry would eventually come around to my way of thinking. Once he realised I could be a good mother, he would be all for it.

I was very serious about keeping Roger. I fixed his room up nicely. I painted it, bought some soft plush toys for him to play with and put little animal pillows in his new crib. I bought a playpen with 'Winnie the Pooh' and all his friends on it. I hung pictures of animals, trucks, cars, and everything, I thought a little boy should have in their room.

I sewed red white and blue curtains, with little toy soldier tie backs. Jerry said I had done a marvellous job.

"I bet Roger never had anything like this in his room, with the foster parents." Jerry was looking around the room as he spoke.

I felt very pleased, and thought Jerry was finally coming around to the idea of having the 'patter of little feet' in the house.

I dreamed that Roger would grow up healthy, and happy, and that Jerry would become a great dad. I would be a patient loving mother, and finally have my picture perfect family.

We finally did it. Roger was our son. We signed the papers and took him home. We waved goodbye to his old home, and hello to his new one. Only this time it was permanent. I spent almost all of my waking hours taking care of Roger. I enjoyed being his mother but it was a lot of hard work. He made me laugh with his antics; he blew bubbles, clapped his hands, and giggled a lot. He sat quietly as I read stories to him, and let me introduce him to all the animals in his room. I tried, sometimes in vain, to make sounds like the animals. He liked it best, when I tried to roar like a lion. It came out as more of a funny growl.

I took pictures of Roger almost every day. When Jerry came home, I begged him to be in the pictures with us. I so wanted Jerry to take a walk with Roger in his stroller, or maybe help me feed, or bath him. But Jerry had taken to working in the yard, or down in the basement. He was spending less and less time with us, and for the most part, ignoring us.

Suddenly, Jerry was not by my side anymore. He had always been there, but when Roger came to live with us, he found other things to do. He never helped with Roger. He didn't want to do anything with him.

Jerry and I were drifting apart.

He began to make plans to go away with what used to be 'our' friends. He told them I didn't have the time, what with the child and all. He became resentful and angry all the time. He slammed doors, and made loud noises. I would ask him not to wake Roger, and he would reply with: "I'm not changing my life for that kid!"

I was devastated. I didn't bother to tell Jerry about the cute little things that Roger was doing. If I did, he would come back with some kind of smart remark. Most of the time his answer was: "If he was like other kids his age, he would have done that already."

I tried to explain to Jerry, if he would just spend some time with Roger, he would feel differently about him. But Jerry would just shrug his shoulders and say: "No way."

Jerry's opinion was that Roger wouldn't get better from his horrible birth but worse as he got older. I felt just the opposite. My frustration grew. I prayed for Jerry to act like Roger's dad. I desperately wanted us to be a real family.

I felt that God had given us Roger as a blessing, but Jerry felt we had been given Roger as a curse from the Devil.

Eventually Jerry became verbally abusive to Roger. He would ignore him when he held out his little arms, for Jerry to take him; Jerry would stare down at him and then walk away.

Jerry started belittling me in front of our guests. He would embarrass me purposely, and make me look like a fool. The silent treatment was becoming the norm in our house.

For a while, I went back to my old routine. It was easy; I had done it for so long in my past life.

I begged him for acceptance. I made him special dinners, and put Roger to bed early. I did everything I could to make Jerry love us.

But thank goodness I came to my senses. I realised, I was following my old habits all over again. I had to break the cycle.

Jerry took to sleeping in the guest room with the door locked. I would knock on the door, and ask if we could talk it over. He would pretend to be sleeping and snore loudly. There was only one thing he forgot, he didn't snore!

From the beginning Roger had only one parent, and that was me. It was obvious to everyone; all our friends said that Jerry was running away from us.

We lived in the house like strangers, never speaking never touching. It was really bad for both of us.

Finally, one afternoon, it all came to a head. Jerry came home early and walked into the house. He began pacing back and forth in front of me.

"All right Jerry, spit it out, say what you have to say." I wanted this talked out.

"I want to take Roger back to the home, this isn't working out." Jerry was serious.

"Roger is our son. We love him, how can you say something like that." I was shocked.

The look on his face told me differently. He didn't love Roger. Even more, I don't think he loved me.

"He ... he ... he isn't my son Darlene. He's, well, if anything, he's yours."

He looked at me with a cold strange look and continued to speak. "Darlene, here's the thing. You have to choose. It's me or Roger."

I looked away for a moment, all the old fears found their way back to the surface. If I told him to go, could I possibly make it on my own with a child? What would happen to me? Oh, God! I would be alone. Not just alone, but with a child to bring up. Is it possible?

I knew at that moment, our marriage was over. Any respect that I had for him, was now gone. Any love that he had for me, had got tangled up in his disdain for Roger.

What was left? Could he and I make it? Should I honour his wishes? I didn't think so. I didn't answer his question, of who I would choose. Not now, not yet. It was too soon. I needed time to think. I didn't know what to do.

I got up and left the room. I went out to the patio. I stood there alone for a long time. Thinking and thinking. What if?

Slowly I went over, every horrible word that had passed between us, over the past months. I couldn't figure out in my mind, why he couldn't be more understanding. Didn't he love me? Didn't he want me to be happy? Didn't he see that happiness to me meant having Roger, and him? I couldn't decide what to do. I didn't know.

I walked back to the house. I went to Roger's room and saw him lying there asleep. He had no idea that his home was about to be torn apart. He slept the sleep of angels, and looked so sweet and lovable. I couldn't give him up. I didn't want to give him up. The problem was, I didn't want to give up Jerry either. What was I to do?

Jerry went to work the next day as usual, and I didn't get up to make his breakfast. I didn't want to face him. I still didn't know what to do. I went through the motions of the day. I fed, walked, and bathed Roger. I hugged him every chance I got, I held him tightly, and then put him to bed early.

Jerry walked in. I looked at him with tears in my eyes. He looked away and put down the evening paper.

"Well, have you made your decision?" He asked with his back to me.

"Yes, I have made my decision." I spoke slowly and carefully weighing the words.

He turned slowly and looked at me. He knew it was over, he just needed to hear me say it.

"Roger and I will be moving out next week." The tears were now flowing down my cheeks. "I'm sorry, Jerry. You didn't give me any other choice." I walked out the front door; I didn't want him to see the pain I was feeling. I didn't want him to hear the hurt in my voice if I had to speak to him.

When I came back into the house, Jerry was in 'his' room, and I in mine. He didn't go to work the next day, but instead went directly to an attorney. They drew up 'no fault' divorce papers and he came directly home. He packed a bag and made his way to the front door.

"May I come back tonight Darlene, and we'll talk?" He asked.

"No Jerry, I would rather you wait until Roger and I have left. That will be next week."

Jerry slammed the door behind him, he never looked back.

Later that night the door bell rang. It was Jerry.

"I want a divorce. I will pay the child support." His words ran together as if they had been rehearsed. He continued. "I want the house Darlene. I wish it had turned out differently, but you wanted it your way. If you want to keep that sick kid, then so be it!"

I started to turn away.

"Will you be OK without me? I mean, you have so many problems of your own. We always worked out your problems together. Didn't we Darlene, didn't we?"

"Um ... well, Roger and I are a good team Jerry, I talk, and he listens."

And that was that.

Chapter Thirteen

On My Own ... Again And Again!

Old habits die hard, I guess. I had talked with Johnny before about my problems with Jerry, and I guess he wasn't all that surprised to hear that Jerry and I, were on the verge of a divorce. I had called him that same night, the night Jerry had asked for the divorce.

"Johnny, I was really surprised that Jerry left the way he did. I don't think he ever loved me, do you?" I asked.

"Sis, here's the thing. You were in the hospital for a long time, between marrying Jerry and actually living with him, that was quite a while. Perhaps ... em ... maybe you just didn't know him as well as you should have. Jerry was a complicated fellow and you were insistent about adopting. Perhaps it was just too early in your relationship to adopt."

"Well, we talked about it for more than a year, before we actually did anything. He had plenty of time to object." I offered.

"Maybe, he didn't think it would actually happen. I don't know. I do know that Jerry wanted to take care of you, and frankly, I can't imagine him leaving you, the way he has. Perhaps it was Roger's infirmity that bothered him. You know Darlene, some people aren't very good at dealing with people who are ... are ... well, you know? *Different*. I don't know ... it's too bad. But that aside sis, you are going back to your counselling, aren't you? And ... well, you know that I love you more than anything, but you have to stop making these mistakes. You trust people too much."

"You might be right Johnny, but at this point, I've got to get out of here."

"You promise to come to me, and get with a good counsellor, right?" He kind of asked but it came out like a statement.

"Yes, I rushed this marriage. I thought I knew him. I just didn't. We wanted different things in our life, and I didn't realise it. Not until he asked me to choose between him and Roger."

"Well, come on out and stay with us for a while. OK?" He asked.

"Yes, I will Johnny. I will."

So I moved to California with Roger in tow, and what little furniture that was mine,

following close behind. I had to find a counsellor and Johnny suggested this Dr Rey-
nolds. She was a 'talk show' host, on a radio
show in the Bakersfield, California area. She
was very popular. I went to her for two long
years ... and then I met Jim.

Not long after I left, I heard from a relative of Jerry's that he had passed away. I
couldn't have been more shocked! When he
left our home, he was in fine shape, but I
suppose things change quickly sometimes. I
asked his relative what he died of, and she
told me he had Lung Cancer! I was stunned.
Jerry had never smoked a cigarette in his
life, nor did he use any kind of tobacco, that
I knew of. I suppose there are some cases,
where the person just has the disease and
dies. I always thought it was smoking
related. According to the relative, he had
'the fast kind'; by the time it was diagnosed
it was too late to do anything about it.

The next thing I knew, I was at a memorial service for poor Jerry. I felt so bad. Had
I only known how ill he was? I really had a
huge guilt issue, and couldn't stop crying
during the service.

I knew Jerry could be a beast, but he had
helped me through so much. I felt so guilty
about him dying, so soon after I left. I was a

little quick to let Jerry go. I told myself it was him that chose to walk out the door, but in all, as I looked back, it was partly me too.

Standing there at his memorial service, I felt really bad that we had parted on such harsh terms. But ... then, there was that horrible argument over Roger. And I just couldn't let our son go back to that orphanage. Jerry just didn't understand my deep feelings about being a mum.

So, even though that chapter of my life was now closed, I did find myself wishing that he had at least contacted me before his death. I would have been with him those last hours. I felt really bad. After all, he had been with me all those years and during that horrible time in the hospital. He did have his good points, he really did. I wept openly for him.

My issues are still right out there, on the front burner, and I'm not sure to this day how to handle them. I can't bring myself to trust people in general, and men in part-icular. That is not a good thing.

There was the case of Jim. He and I just didn't hit it off at the beginning. Perhaps it was issues of trust with me, or perhaps it was my female intuition. Either way, I know

I should have paid more attention to my misgivings than I did.

Then, talk about odd, out of the clear blue my missing mother appeared on the scene. And with her, she brought a whole slew of other relatives that I really hadn't known before.

It had been years since I had seen her. She didn't come around when I was in the hospital. Not even when there was talk of me not surviving, being thrown off the cliff. In fact, since I moved from the Midwest the first time, I hadn't seen or heard much from her at all.

We talked, and I guess we made up for lost time. We connected on several different levels, and we did become close rather quickly. She did finally bother to explain, why she left Johnny and me so very long ago. She seemed sincere when she told me that she and dad, just weren't seeing eye to eye. She also explained why so many things had gotten her down. She said that was the real reason she picked up and left. But to me, the amazing thing was, that she never mentioned her long dark days, of manic depression. She didn't mention the horrible crying days, that seemed to me, to last forever.

So really, after all this time, she was still less than forthcoming about her life away from us. She never spoke in any detail about what she did, after she left us. There was no explanation as to why; she didn't come back for Johnny and me.

Those questions are still unanswered, even to this day.

There is one thing for certain; she has never sought any professional help. In my opinion, that would have helped her so very much.

She has never to this day, ever talked about her abrupt departure from our lives. But, we decided to get along.

I had missed my mother something fierce for the last twenty-five years. I wanted to get back with her, and try to understand her.

Jim and I married. Yes, that's the guy I didn't hit it off with straight away. He has two children himself from his first marriage. They were barely teenagers when I moved in with them. As teenagers can be, they were a little out of hand. However, slowly, as they got used to me, they became more receptive to my correcting them. We all took a while to adjust to each other.

Jim is a very good man and a very good father to his children. Seeing this in him, I decided to enquire if I could adopt another child. He was very receptive to the idea.

We adopted a boy. So now there were two young boys, an older boy, and an older girl.

Jim was very accepting of the situation, and seemed for a long while, to be accepting me, and my sometimes weird behaviour.

When I feel pressured, by finances, the kids, or the marriage, I freak out. My mouth goes off, and I say things that are hurtful and can't be taken back.

Then there are the anxieties that I live with, on a daily basis. And those, coupled with my other problems, can be a handful.

Jim took this all in stride for a long, long time. The boys enjoyed the interaction with the older kids, and seemingly they enjoyed the chaos of each other for a while.

Jim's determination was the only thing holding our marriage together. We would have times when our ideas of parenting were totally at odds. We struggled through, and worked it out, and worked it out, and worked it out.

To tell you the absolute truth, I really didn't hold out much hope for this marriage.

Not from the beginning, not from the middle, and well, you get the picture.

At this time because of the 'cliff thing' in Alaska, the doctor's tell me there is some scar tissue, forming behind one of my ears. They have also told me the 'bad' news. They explained that in time, this scar tissue would lead to seizures!

Well, with the memory loss problem, and this looming in my future, I had to apply for SSI Disability. I hated the very idea of this.

Then, on top of everything else, my B.S. in accounting that I had worked so hard for, was useless. Because of the 'cliff' thing and the memory problem, the degree simply hangs on my wall and is of no use to any-one, particularly me! You have to remember what you were taught.

While there is always hope that I will fully recover, I can put my thoughts down on paper. I can also raise my kids. But I liked to work, and being at home is nerve racking to me.

I used to love getting out and talking to people, meeting new friends and all of that.

Even now, my memory still plays tricks on me. I have these flashes that come to me, just like pictures playing in my mind. I used to take them at face value, and think that they were really another part of my memory coming back to me. But after talking with relatives and friends that were around at the time the memory was, I find that sometimes they are just flashes. When I find out that certain flashes are my memory returning, I get really excited, and that helps me a great deal!

And then something weird happened.

Jerry showed up!

Now I don't know how you would react, to a supposed dead ex-husband showing up in the middle of your new life. But I was absolutely freaked out, by the situation! I didn't know what to do.

I couldn't believe my ears; I thought someone was playing a practical joke on me. But there he was, as large as life, and talking to me on my phone. I didn't know what to say, I was dumbstruck. I was listening to him but all the while I was thinking, *I am not a widow, I am not a widow, I am not a widow.*

I hadn't done anything with the divorce papers, Jerry had drawn up in Florida the night he left. One of the main reasons being, I had very little money. I thought I would wait until I got settled in California, and then deal with it. Then I got the phone call, to say Jerry was dead. I had gone to his Memorial service, and even talked to his Doctor.

So I think you could understand, why I saw no reason to divorce a dead man!

But well, now, here he was alive!

Apparently, he tracked me down by calling my mother. He knew that I was going to California, so he simply figured out how to find me.

The long and the short of it is, I had began writing my life story and hired an agent.

She was in the midst of putting my story together in order to present it to the movie, and TV producers. I was very happy about the prospects, and told everyone, as you would, including Jerry when he was alive. He seemed happy for me at the time, so I didn't think any more about it.

Then he proceeded to tell me on the phone what he had done, and why he had been presumed dead!

"Well Darlene. This friend of mine introduced me to a friend of his, a woman. We got to talking, and I don't know what really happened, but one thing lead to another, and well, I moved in with her for a while."

"Oh Really!" I replied.

"Yes. Anyhow, she told me about this friend of hers who was really out of money. They found a doctor that was pretty much on the shady side, and they made a deal.

The doctor would be on a certain street, at a certain time, and her friend would drive out in front of an on-coming truck, or car. The doctor would then rush over and take this woman's pulse, and pronounce her as being dead!"

"Dead Jerry! What good would that do anyone?" I asked like a fool, I just didn't get it.

"Well, oh, I forgot to say, her friend had taken out a huge insurance policy about six months before that. Anyhow, this doctor pronounced her dead and then called this funeral home. They came out and picked up her body. The woman had arranged for another friend of hers, to get the insurance money, and they split it."

"Sounds like a good way to get a jail sentence to me Jerry." I said.

"Yeah, well, they have to catch you first. Anyways, so I got to thinking about it. I mean, you weren't there, we were getting a divorce, and I didn't have any reason to go on. So I went and bought this two million dollar policy on myself, and took this friend of mine, and she pretended to be you. I bought a million dollar policy on her too, just to make it look good. Then four months ago, I died."

211

"I know that Jerry, your niece called me. I wept for you Jerry, I really did. I felt bad because I wasn't there with you. And all this time, you were fine! How could you do that? I ... I ... how could you do such a thing Jerry?" I started crying as if he were dead.

"I didn't think Darlene. Truly I didn't. I am so stupid; I forgot that you would have to know. And ... well, I'm sorry Darlene, I am truly sorry. Anyway, all that aside, I'm a millionaire! I want us to get back together. We will meet in one of them South American Countries, and buy a house and live like royalty for the rest of our lives."

"Jerry, you're crazy, you have lost the plot, think about it. This is my new home, I'm married, I love Jim, and we are going to adopt another child. What on earth are you thinking about?"

"I know Darlene; he's got a pack of kids. He can keep all of them, and we can go to South America. I mean to say, that seems fair. Don't you think? We can have the life! The American dream, we can have it all. I mean, Darlene think about it. I have over a million dollars and we can live any way, or in any place, we want. Just you and me honey, like it should have been all along." He begged.

"Jerry, Roger and I can't leave. I just can't leave Jim and the new child. This is what I want. I want to raise kids, and make them feel like they are wanted and loved. I want them to feel like they have a place in my life. Don't you realise that? I want a family. Money doesn't mean that much to me. If I can't have children, there is no point to anything for me. Jerry, you are wasting your time asking me to leave. I will not go with you. My answer is NO!!

Jerry told me he was phoning from the neighbourhood, and asked if he could stay for a while. I know it sounds crazy, but Jim and I put him up in our spare room.

I went off to see about some personal business, and Jim was at work. The house was empty, except for Jerry. I really didn't think that much about leaving him there alone. After all, we had been married for years.

While we were all out, he searched through my private desk and found my agent's name and telephone number. He called her up the same morning. He told her he was representing me and that she could go ahead and buy us out. We would step back from any deal that she might have going on! Luckily, she was a person that was on the up and up, and she did nothing until she talked to me personally. And of course, I had no idea that he had even called her.

So there he was, a liar and a crook!

I thought that Jerry was a number of things, but I never would have believed that he was an out and out crook. He had stolen the money from the insurance company, and then tried to extort money from my agent. It's a true saying, you never know people, even if you live with them for years. He had left right after he phoned the agent.

A couple of weeks later, my mother called me.

"Did you see in the paper where Jerry died?" She asked.

"What?"

"Did you see in the paper where your husband Jerry died?" She repeated herself.

"Again! You mean he has died again?"

"No, it's for real this time Darlene. He was driving on the freeway and pulled over to the side of the road. He died right there on the spot. The Police came, and it was on the TV. Anyhow, he's really dead this time!"

"Thanks for letting me know momma, I had better get off the phone and find out what I can." I hung up and grabbed the phone book.

This was a horrible time. Jerry had died for real. He died with no money on him, except a few dollars. He had no banking account and he was in danger of being buried in a paupers' grave. I had no way of knowing where the money was from the insurance company. I didn't even know the name of the woman who had helped him pull off the deal.

So there I was. I felt I should take the responsibility of holding the service, and burying Jerry. I didn't know where to bury him, so I thought California would be as good a place as any. He didn't have any real relatives that I knew of, except a niece in Kentucky. I called her and told her that Jerry was really gone this time, and she was amazed. Apparently she thought, as we all had, that he was really dead the first time.

We got through the funeral, and I was able to say a proper goodbye to Jerry.

Things are difficult; no one ever said that 'life' was going to be easy. That much I can attest to. But when after five years you are faced with making a decision that will be best for you, it is more than difficult, it is nearly impossible. But, you forge ahead and make that decision.

I am a well known chicken!

215

I tried to make excuses, to cover up my real feelings, and tried to 'go along', just to keep the peace. I am here to tell you, it just doesn't work! I had to decide whether I was going to stay in the relationship with Jim, or call it quits! So, for months, I opted to stay. I tried to explain what I felt was wrong between him and I. I also tried to excuse my own actions, and then made excuses for his reactions.

I am sorry to say, it didn't work.

And so, I moved away.

I miss the beautiful green of the Midwest, and the rolling hills of Missouri and Arkansas. I have found a home near my little brother Johnny, and I feel good about the move. Jim wasn't at fault, I wasn't either. We just have different ideas about love, marriage and the raising of the children.

Most of all perhaps, it's time that Darlene depended upon herself, to make it through this world, and not on someone else to make it for her. I have some dreams, and I think they will come true this time.

I have had a real growing experience. That is; I have come to realise, that I can't go through this life blaming everyone else for my problems. I have to look my life square in the face, and continue to grow. I have to do that alone for a while.

So, on to my new home, and our new life.

Sometimes it is very difficult to believe that there is life after such extreme abuse, as I have suffered. But there is. In a way, the sad part is, that the victim is never the same. But then, on the other hand, it would be tragic, if I were the same person. I trusted everyone to make my decisions for me, and that was wrong. I got in to all kinds of trouble with this attitude. The thing that I have learned from all of this, is, that everything takes time. I will, I hope, someday trust people, and hopefully men again. I will at some point let the walls down between me and the rest of the world.

I also now realise, it will take years to completely recover from being thrown off that cliff. Perhaps longer before I stop freaking out at smells, sounds, flashes or even memories.

As victims, we always have incidents that bring back memories, and certainly not all of them are good. The best thing you can do, in my opinion, is give everything time and pray that our loved ones understand and support us.

I will continue counselling, and I would recommend that to anyone who is a victim

217

of anything in their lives.

I would also like to say, never, never, blame yourself. You are the VICTIM. You must remember that.

Do what you can to get up every morning with a smile. Take the day as it comes and give it all you have. Grieving, guilt, feeling sad and angry, all take time and energy. Healing, whether it is physical or mental, will take as long as it takes. Some of us will get over things in a year, and some of us will get over things in ten years, or twenty-years, who knows?

It has been thirteen years for me, and although things get easier, it doesn't really fade from my memory. I hope that this book will make it easier for someone else, and me.

Chapter Fourteen

Get Help

As my story closes, I would like to say a few other things. To those of you who are either in this type of abusive relationship, or who may know of someone who is living in this kind of hell.

The first thing is: do what I say, not what I do! In other words, this suggestion comes from my own personal experience, and does not reflect what I actually did.

You should immediately get help from a qualified person, if you are a victim of any type of abuse. Whether it is verbal or physical.

Get your children out of the home. It is **not** better to keep the family unit together for the children's sake. THAT IS UTTER HOGWASH!

When you stay in an abusive relationship, you are not kidding anyone except yourself. You are in danger. You could be killed during one of the fights. If you don't believe me, check with any professional person who has counselled, or dealt with people who live with abuse. They will tell you that statistics show the shocking truth. Out of three women who live in an abusive home, two of them will die. Sometimes the death is an accident, and sometimes it is not. Either way, dead is dead!

If you know anyone that is being abused, reach out and help them. Tell someone. Tell anyone, and eventually someone will step in and help.

If you see or hear your own children imitating the abuser to another child, or to you. Stop them immediately. Don't allow the cycle of abuse to continue.

And, may I make a personal plea. If you have time to volunteer at your local abuse centre, please do so. If you have some extra money that you would like to contribute to a charity. Please make out a cheque, no matter how small, and drop it in the mail to your local *Domestic Violence Centre*.

Domestic violence is a problem, not only here in the United Kingdom and the United States but worldwide. We must all do what we can to stop it. Remember, if not you, then who?

The 'NATIONAL DOMESTIC VIOLENCE' helpline number for the UK is:
0808 2000247

The 'NATIONAL DOMESTIC VIOLENCE' helpline number for the USA is:
1-800-799-7233

If you are in present danger in the UK, call **999**.

If you are in present danger in the USA, call **911**.

If you are a teenager and are in a violent relationship: GET OUT!

If your boyfriend or girlfriend is possessive of you and your time, this is a warning sign!

If your boyfriend or girlfriend pressures you to have sex: GET OUT!

We women tend to go back into a relationship if he brings us flowers, and apologises. He says he's sorry. He is. He is a sorry individual, and you need to: GET OUT!

Remember my cliff incident?

I really should stop saying incident. I should say. "REMEMBER MY EX-HUSBAND HIRED TWO MEN TO MURDER ME."

I just can't stress to you enough, how important it is for you to get out of an abusive relationship.

Don't ask. "Why doesn't she just leave?" Ask. "What can I do to help her, or him?"

If we can fund more agencies to provide more information on this subject to the general public, more people in the court system, and the police, will understand what is going on.

Epilogue

The following is a story that appeared in the Springdale, Arkansas newspaper regarding my kidnapping:

SPRINGDALE MAN SENTENCED FOR 5 COUNTS OF ATTEMPTED MURDER AND KIDNAPPING!

By Julie Cameron/Staff writer Ozark

A local man accused of kidnapping his wife and attempting to murder her and several police deputies is awaiting trial. Bobby Fulton hobbled into court and sat behind the defense attorney.
He sat silently with his head down throughout the proceedings.
The end of the court hearings found Bobby Fulton guilty and sentenced to life without parole to serve at the prison for the criminally insane.

My ex- husband Bobby Fulton was given a jail sentence of twenty years to life without parole. This was to be served at a hospital for the criminally insane. The judge felt he was a harm to himself and society. Due to the extent of the abuse imposed on me, the impregnating of two minors, and pulling a gun on the sheriff's officers.

One of my sisters-in-law sadly took her own life.

The church that we belonged to, the 'Bible Church', met the following end:

LOCAL GROUP OF CHURCHES DISAPPEAR

By Thomas Laird/Staff Writer

Local group of churches have their organisation dissolved and doors closed. Due to a federal and state investigation it has been established that funds for the organisation were mishandled as well as rumours of minors being abused by elders of the church.

Several parties have been detained with charges pending in reference to misappropriation of funds, tax evasion, and abuse.

The church has been dissolved due to a government investigation that uncovered

many illegal acts, of which; the raping of young girls was at the forefront.
There were several that were incarcerated for embezzlement and are now serving jail time.

Aunt Loretta died of old age.

Two of my ex-brothers-in-law were jailed for various reasons.

Only one of the brothers' has been able to establish a fairly good life, and is in counselling. He has a good job and has been clean of alcohol for some years.

And so, this is the end of my story. I really should say it is the beginning.

My children and I are living on a good sized acreage, and I am growing roses. We have returned to the Midwest, and I am becoming re-acquainted with my sister. You know her as 'Laura'. I am also getting to know my older brother 'Jackie', and my younger brother, 'Johnny'. We are getting together regularly now, and becoming a real family unit.

My brother 'Johnny' is now living back in the Midwest, with his new wife and their two children. He is a fireman.

My sister and her husband live not too far from me, and this is a blessing. She really likes my kids and is helping me with them, from time to time. She and I are hoping to start our own small business soon. Her husband has just returned from Iraq.

My mother and I have reunited, and she is coming to live with the rest of the family in the Midwest in a few months.

And me ... well, things are being told to me about my earlier life, and I'm sort of mixing them in with my own memory. I am feeling really good about myself and my little family at the moment.

I'm doing well physically, and I think I'm doing very well mentally. And *'day after day I'm getting better and better'*. Trust me when I tell you. If you too get out of your situation, then you too will be able to say, *'day after day I'm getting better and better'*!

My love and prayers are with you.

Those memory flashes slowly became an entire story and now it is done. The book is finished, so will be my entire past.

And I, well, I am on the way to becoming a very happy lady.

Thank you for reading my story and remember, if you have some extra time on your hands, please donate it to a *'domestic violence centre'*. You will be helping some-

one, and think how good you will feel about
yourself.

Thank you for buying my book.
You are helping me in my recovery.

People, who bought Darlene's book, also bought the following:

A STONE IN MY SHOE
ISBN: 1904762301 ISBN: 9781904762300
£15.99 $29.95 Hardback

SAFE CONDUCT
ISBN: 1904762093 ISBN: 9781904762096
£8.99 $16.95 Paperback

Our books are available from all good book-stores world wide.
Don't forget, you can also order our books from your local library.

Why not visit our website and see our whole selection of books.
www.lipstickpublishing.com

COMING SOON:
PRECIOUS TIMES:
ISBN: 1904762255 ISBN: 9781904762256
£7.99 $14.95 Paperback

LIPSTICK PUBLISHING
www.lipstickpublishing.com